Contents

Preface

1 Doubting Abbey

"Why won't you allow us to be blessed?"

Those words stabbed my heart. It was a question I had never fully considered. My family had fallen on hard times, and we were in need. A family at church offered money to help with bills, and even though they were good friends of ours, my pride always led me to say, "No, thank you. We'll figure something out." One Sunday morning, while standing in the church lobby, he again offered two thousand dollars. As usual, I turned him down. Only this time, it was different. After my refusal, he gently grabbed my left forearm; and with tears welling up in his eyes, he said, "Why won't you allow us to be blessed? We're trying to help. We want to help, and it would be a blessing to us to help you. But you won't allow us to be blessed. Why?"

Those words and the look on his face hurt my soul. I immediately knew it was incumbent on me to evaluate my heart and the wholly destructive nature of pride. Being dependent on someone else was new to me. In my heart, and mind, being in need was unmanly—and embarrassing, not just embarrassing to the members of my family. In my eyes, I was personally an embarrassment to my wife and kids. From my perspective, taking financial help clearly meant "Dad can't take care of us. Dad is a failure." No father, no dad, ever wants to hear that, let alone think it. Above all else, taking care of your family is the ultimate responsibility of a father, and I was failing miserably.

I had always taken pride in having worn-out gloves. Worn-out gloves meant I was willing to work. It meant I would reach beyond normal wear and tear and outwork the person next to me, no matter the task.

It would not be considered grand to someone of excessive wealth, but to me, I had built a small "Camelot" for my family. Through hard work, I had a successful golf design business. I had money, famous friends, forty acres of land north of Dallas, a large house, a pool, a big fertile garden, and longhorn cattle. We had everything we needed, and there was no want. I felt exceedingly blessed by God, almost as if he was rewarding my worn-out gloves.

My family was active in the church. I was a deacon on several committees, taught many classes, and occasionally preached. My wife and I started a successful Christian academy. My children were strong and able fixtures at school, in the community, and in the youth group at church. For all intents and purposes, we had the world by the tail, until one day.

It was the Tuesday morning we all remember. Serious questions immediately sprung to mind when the first plane hit the World Trade Center. "What kind of plane was it?" "How could that happen?" "Could that have possibly been intentional?" The unthinkable even began to surface. "Is the United States under attack?" All doubt was erased when the next plane hit the other World Trade Center tower. The United States was under attack. September 11, 2001, was a horrible day that literally changed the world forever. Blatant and intentional evil had proudly and spectacularly shown its ugly head.

You would not guess the events of that day would have a serious impact on the golf industry, but they did. The nation's economy took a turn for the worse, and when that happens, the first thing people do is cut back on nonessential expenses. Entertainment is at the top of that list, and to a struggling family, golf is definitely considered a nonessential expense. Rounds of golf played dropped sharply throughout the United States. Interestingly, in addition to the bad economy, the drop in play was driven in part by a fear of flying. Obviously, golf courses and resorts depend on people vacationing and traveling to their site. For a period of time after 9/11, people were afraid to fly for fear of another hijacking. Many people simply cancelled plans for air travel. The drop in the golf economy put many golf development projects on hold, decimating the golf course architecture community. Simply put, the jobs went away. This downturn in the golf industry lasted two to three years. Then, in 2004–2005, things began to rebound as the economy and housing markets gradually regained strength. Golf developments slowly resurfaced, and golf architecture was again prosperous.

As my family made serious financial commitments in 2000, the unexpected downturn from 2001 to 2004 put us in a significant financial hole. Even though we struggled mightily to make ends meet, I never felt a loss of support from my wife and children. In fact, many times they were the positive reinforcement I needed to keep moving forward.

The return of design work in 2004–2005 was a godsend. I had good jobs that generated travel to exciting parts of the world I had always longed to visit. By 2008, our design tables were full with projects in Texas, Illinois, Idaho, California, Mexico, and China. Money started rolling in with lucrative design fees. We not only were able to get out of debt incurred during the 2001–2005 downturn but also were beginning to set money aside for our kids' future college expenses and our eventual retirement. Our financial future looked extremely bright.

The first sign of some trouble came in early September of 2008 with a gentle flutter in the stock market. However, the real trouble started on September 15 when Lehman Brothers filed for bankruptcy. Not only was this bank considered "too big to fail" but also they were providing the funding for our new golf resort development project in Cabo San Lucas, Mexico. When Lehman Brothers collapsed, global financial markets went into freefall. By the end of October 2008, a full financial meltdown was in place, and every one of our projects had come to a screeching halt. In a short span of six weeks, we went from being flush with jobs and income to having no work and no income at all. And, to make it worse, all the financial experts in the world had no idea how bad things would get or how long the downturn would last.

October of 2008 was the start of what our family calls "the lean years." I can't remember who coined the term, but it was gentler than calling them "the years of implosion." To say the least, the years since 2008 have been difficult. The days of worn-out gloves instead became sleepless nights of prayer on worn-out knees.

When experiencing such difficult times, you tend to have one of two reactions toward God. One is to turn your back on him in anger and doubt. The other is to turn to him in complete faith and obedience. Ironically, I have found the two reactions can occur not only in the same day; they can happen in the same prayer. Trial and tribulation is a violent emotional, spiritual, psychological, and physical roller coaster, especially when it involves a wife and children. They are innocent casualties that cause the deepest searing pain.

My entire life had been lived going to church on Sunday mornings and Wednesday nights. Faith was assumed, but maybe never given a true birth complete with my specific DNA. Without realizing it, we as "Christians" so often live off the faith of our parents and grandparents. It isn't until experiencing lean years that we begin to look deeply into a faith often best described as "a storm." Some days are clear and offer the serenity of a long vision, while others are days of clouds, lightning, and a cold rain that soaks the depth of your soul.

On a roller coaster, everyone takes their seat with anticipation and excitement. The ride is designed to create drama as it slowly takes you to a high precipice. From this elevated vantage point, the magnificent view is far-reaching, and you are full of excitement. But the fall is coming. You hear the loud "clickety-clack" of the chain as anticipation builds for the huge drop ahead. You look at the person seated next to you and share the combined look of trepidation and exhilaration. Your compartment rolls over the edge of the high point, and you start to fall. Centrifugal force takes over, and your stomach feels like it has slammed into your throat. Your esophagus and tongue are fighting for the same space in your mouth. The screams of other riders are muffled by the intestines wrapped around your head; you assume the intestines are yours. You pick up speed. It is a time of sheer dread and fear. But, in the back of your mind, your fear is calibrated because you know the fall is temporary. You know there is soon coming a time when the ride changes course and you start to ascend. You say to yourself, "If I can just make it through the fall, I will enjoy the rest of the ride."

What would it be like if you lacked the confidence that the rise was coming after the fall? Would you be as excited to get on the ride in the first place?

The lean years of life can often feel long and exhausting as you wait confidently for the ascension. Over time, that confidence can devolve to hope, and hope can descend into doubt. Doubt, discouragement, and depression are where Satan seems to live and do his best work. If you could catch a glimpse of Satan's business card, I think you would see his address is "1 Doubting Abbey."

I read somewhere that "Satan wants you to concentrate on the pain of your past, while God wants you to concentrate on the glorious future that awaits." This simple sentence is powerful. Satan desires us to dwell in pain, hurt, discouragement, and doubt. God desires us to live in joy, hope, faith, and obedience.

Joy in the midst of a storm—how can that be?

There are two passages from the Bible that have intrigued me in these lean years: James 1:2–8 and Habakkuk 3:17–19. I have turned to them for uplifting strength and encouragement, but have also read them many times seemingly sitting alone on a cold bench in Satan's playground of doubt and disbelief. I have read them and come away with pure joy. I have also read them and come away with pure discouragement.

The joy comes from the encouragement and hope resting within these texts. They overflow with a God relationship and a glorious future. The discouragement comes from the fact that I sometimes feel so far from the ideals of these passages. I see them, I read them, and I believe them; but I am simply not there. I feel so far from the peace, joy, and calm they have to offer; and I struggle with "Why? Why am I not there?"

I am not a theologian or preacher. I am just a simple golf course architect who has traveled the globe for the last twenty-nine years building two hundred-acre playgrounds of grass, sand, and water. I have been richly blessed to see some of the most beautiful sceneries in the world and to work with a wide variety of people in many different cultures. I have spent countless hours in airports, on planes, and in rental cars, followed by innumerable lonely meals and nights in distant hotels. Through the years, I have had much time to read the Bible, think, ponder, and wonder. I have often called it "wondering while wandering."

The story is personally painful. I have reluctantly told some people, and each time I have been met with the same reaction, "You have got to tell this story. There are so many people who need to hear it." When I hear that, I wonder, *Why? Why would someone need to hear this?*

It seems we are all searching, but I wonder if we know what we are searching for. Satan has done such a masterful job at making us want and desire and always feeling like we are missing out on something. Satan desires us to be in need and discontent. I have found "contentment" to be an elusive ideal.

This book is about a sinner's roller-coaster ride that has not yet returned to the loading platform, where all the other eager riders wait. This book is an ongoing journey through lean years as I strive for the relationship with God that he desires. It is a journey while seeking contentment. The journey has had many times of complete sorrow and tears and many times with a full measure of joy or laughter. You may relate to the journey. If so, I hope it reaches your heart and draws you closer to God.

Worn-out gloves

Chapter 1

Lost

"I just feel lost."

- She watches as the casket is slowly lowered into the cold February ground. Inseparable since they were teenagers, they had been married for sixty-one years. Life will never be the same. Loneliness.

- He wakes in the morning, but for the first time in eighteen years, he has no job to go to. Like so many others during the economic downturn of 2008, he has been laid off. What will he do with this day? Life will never be the same. Purposeless.

- She cries as she tells him it was a terrible mistake and only happened once, but infidelity and mistrust have entered the marriage. She desperately pleads for forgiveness, but that thought has abandoned his heart. Life will never be the same. Anger.

- They sit in disbelief as the doctor tells them their beautiful seven-year-old daughter has a rare form of cancer and the chance of survival is heartbreakingly low. Life will never be the same. Mourning.

- He walks across the stage and receives his diploma. From the age of five until this day at the age of twenty-two, he has always been a student. Now, it is all different. Life will never be the same. Anxiety.

Without asking permission

- Life has changed.
- The rules have changed.
- The world has changed.
- Certainty is gone.

"I just feel lost."

Have you ever heard someone say that? Have you ever said it yourself? Things that are familiar and dependable are gone. Uncertainty and anxiety have overtaken your life, as you worry about ever getting to the other side of this. You don't know where to go or what to do next. From this moment forward, your life will never be the same again.

Have you ever felt betrayed by the world? Have you ever felt betrayed by God?

I admit I struggled with that feeling for many years. My world, my family's world, had been turned upside down; and I saw myself as only a colossal failure. Like a castaway on a desert island to a passing airplane, I was screaming and waving my arms at God, but it appeared he was not paying any attention to me and my family. Answers were nonexistent. The rules of life had changed without first asking permission.

This feeling, this phase of life, is actually a very common and well-studied phenomenon. Psychologists refer to it as "liminal space," and loosely defined, it describes a time where circumstances have changed and you are entering an unknown transformational time in life. Interestingly, while most immediately associate it with difficult times when dealing with tragedy or pain, liminal space, and not knowing what lies ahead, can also be associated with times of excitement, fulfillment, hope, and joy.

- He walks across the stage and receives his diploma. From the age of five until this day at the age of twenty-two, he has always been a student. He has graduated and cannot wait to get started with his career. Life will never be the same. Excitement.

- They have known each other since high school and dated for five years. They are still young and unsure of life. They have waited and planned and saved, and she devotedly acts surprised when he drops to his knee with her ring in his hand. He laughs as she says "Yes!" before he can finish the question. Life will never be the same again. Love.

- Contractions are strong, and the doctor is telling her to "Push!" She is strong while rhythmically breathing through the pain. He is acting strong while valiantly trying not to faint. They have wanted a child for so long, and now the day has finally come. Life will never be the same. Joy.

- He worked at the architectural firm for eleven years and designed wonderful buildings and parks, but under the controlling direction of the two partners. He wants to design based on his style and personality. He turns in his two-week notice, files new incorporation papers, and begins talking with people he hopes will become clients. This is a very risky step, but it is his dream. Life will never be the same again. Anticipation.

- She watches as the casket is slowly lowered into the cold February ground. Inseparable since they were teenagers, they had been married for sixty-one years. The last four years had been especially difficult as he suffered with lung and liver cancer. While she is heartbroken and worried about how she will live without him, she is glad his debilitating pain is finally over. She believes he is in heaven worshipping their beloved heavenly Father, and she hopes to see him there one day soon. Life will never be the same. Relief...and hope.

Liminal space. A time of sorrow and anxiety. A time of joy and excitement. A time of transformation.

A quick internet search provides many descriptions and philosophies about liminal space. My attention was drawn to this particular article:

What Is A Liminal Space?

The word *liminal* comes from the Latin word limen, meaning threshold—any point or place of entering or beginning. A liminal space is the time between the "what was" and the "next." It is a place of transition, waiting, and not knowing.

Liminal space is where all transformation takes place, if we learn to wait and let it form us.

Author and theologian Richard Rohr describes this space as:

Where we are betwixt and between the familiar and the completely unknown. There alone is our old world left behind, while we are not yet sure of the new existence. That's a good space where genuine newness can begin. Get there often and stay as long as you can by whatever means possible...This is the sacred space where the old world is able to fall apart, and a bigger world is revealed. If we don't encounter liminal space in our lives, we start idealizing normalcy. The threshold is God's waiting room. Here we are taught openness and patience as we come to expect an appointment with the divine Doctor.

These thresholds of waiting and not knowing our "next" are everywhere in life and they are inevitable. Each ushers in a new chapter of life and holds varying degrees of disruption.

Change never exists in a box, no matter how hard we might try to contain it. Change in one area of life always spills into others that disrupt the status quo. There is a ripple effect. Community, spirituality, vocation, relationships, physicality, friendships and emotions do not exist mutually exclusive from one another—they intersect and intertwine.

When we become aware of our own liminality, most of us, if we're honest, don't know who to become or how to navigate the transition. We often miss the real potential of "in-between" places—we either stand paralyzed or we flee the "terrible cloud of unknown."

If our liminal spaces are approached intentionally and within community, rather than staying paralyzed, running away or going at it alone, we can boldly approach it and confidently move forward into our futures.[1]

Times of transition. The rules have changed. The comfort of certainty has given way to the confusion of uncertainty.

Old World "Certainty"   Time of Transition "Liminal Space"   New World "Uncertainty"

I was drawn to this description of liminal space for five reasons:

---

[1] inaliminalspace.org. liminal space, finding life between chapters. ©2016, Liminal Space/website

1. "Liminal space is where all transformation takes place, if we learn to wait and let it form us." Our natural desire, especially as men, is to try to fix things immediately, which is really just trying to get things back to our comfort zone, where things are certain and under our control. The author is suggesting we enter liminal space with the attitude that I can be transformed into something more than I am now, if I will let this time on the Potter's wheel form me into the image he desires.

2. The author describes liminal space, or the threshold, as "God's waiting room. Here we are taught openness and patience as we come to expect an appointment with the divine Doctor." The threshold is a place of entering. We are entering the waiting room of God, where we hope we will be given answers or a prescription to regain health and vitality. Waiting. A chance to trust? A time to obey?

3. The author openly states that there are different levels of disruption. The life transition of a college graduate heading off to his first job is certainly not as disruptive as that of a father of three young children losing his wife, children, and mother-in-law to a sudden and unexpected death on a November highway north of Dallas. Both are transitions into an unknown, but the father's world is completely and utterly devastated, and he must have community to survive it all.

4. We are not experiencing our times of transition in a box. Times of change can feel very lonely. We often fight it. We often ask, "Why?" We question ourselves and wonder if we brought this on ourselves, while shame and embarrassment become our quicksand. While we may feel completely alone, our situation impacts many people around us—our spouse, children, family, friends, co-workers, and so on. Do we lean on them and seek strength in community, or

do we shut them out and create a chasm that divides and leaves them and us on separate islands of despair?

5. Approach with community. The journey through transition is much easier, or some would say only possible, when you are in a community that cares for you and will offer help, love, and support.

It has been said, "The only constant is change." Times of uncertainty and wondering what lies ahead. It may be good, or it may be bad, but one thing is inescapable: You will experience liminal space. Once that threshold is crossed, the question begins, "How does your outlook, your attitude, your community, and your faith impact the kind of person you will be on the other side?"

In the words of the famous Western author Louis L'Amour, "There will come a time in your life when you think everything is finished. Yet that will be the beginning."

To be continued...

Chapter 2

Three Thorns

Sometimes, you walk through the threshold of your liminal space, but you don't recognize it until years later. I apologize about the length of this chapter, but it is important to understand why this book is even being written. This chapter is mainly the story of our trials since 2008. It does not include any of the times of laughter and immense joy that will be written about later. This story simply highlights the basics of the rise and fall we have experienced.

*****

It is never easy to talk about failure in life.

When someone hears our story, they note the economic downturn was unpredictable and my highly specialized career made finding work especially difficult. Those points are valid, but don't negate the reality of struggle and hardship, particularly involving your wife and children.

In 1983, I enrolled at Lubbock (Texas) Christian College (LCC) to play baseball and earn a biology degree to eventually propel me to medical school and orthopedic surgery. The Lubbock Christian baseball team had just won the 1983 NAIA National Championship, and the biology department was very highly regarded. While at LCC, I met and married a beautiful girl named April. I am convinced God knew life's road that lay before me and the need of a strong helpmate. Little did I know God was supplying the strongest reservoir of faith and love he had to offer.

April and I got married before our senior year, and it was also the year I decided against becoming a doctor and instead planned to get a degree in landscape architecture to design golf courses. When I told April, confusion came over her face as this career departure was a surprise and she knew nothing about landscape architecture. She thought it was mowing lawns and planting bushes. With apprehension, she asked, "So you want to plant bushes?" In her mind, I was switching from being an orthopedic surgeon to a bush planter. I told her I just didn't think God was calling me toward being a doctor and golf course architecture involved design, construction, and travel. Still not understanding, she said, "If that's what you want to do, I'm all for it." That was the beginning of a long line of unwavering support.

I spent the next three years at Texas Tech working toward a landscape architecture degree. To make ends meet, April worked at a dentist's office, and I owned a lawn care business mowing thirty-plus yards a week. However, as grass was dormant, winters were very tough financially. We survived on a weekly regimen of scrambled eggs, tomato soup, hot dog weenies, and venison provided by a friend. Sunday after church was our day to splurge at Bob York's Western Sizzlin' where we would split the #12 Ranger Burger and fries and fill up on unlimited fresh hot rolls delivered throughout the dining room.

Upon graduation from Texas Tech, we moved to Arizona to start my golf architecture career. I was blessed to work with the Scottsdale-based firm of Graham & Panks International (GPI), which was a partnership between 1981 US Open Champion David Graham and golf course architect Gary Panks. At GPI, I was extremely fortunate to work on many high-profile projects around the United States and internationally in Australia, Mexico, Thailand, Canada, Germany, and Indonesia.

The job was good, and we were making a name for ourselves as *Golf World* magazine named us one of the hottest golf design teams in the world. We hobnobbed with famous golfers and celebrities and worked for important government leaders in foreign countries. We flew first class, stayed in five-star hotels, and played prestigious golf courses around the world. By the world's standards, life was very good.

April and I enjoyed our life in Arizona. The weather was wonderful, and the scenery was beautiful. We bought our first house. At 1,667 square feet, we asked, "What will we ever do with this much room?" We found a good church home and made many friends. We were growing in spirit and truth and size with the birth of our three sons: Garrett, Jacob, and Brooks.

In 1996, our family moved back to Texas to open a satellite office in the Dallas area. Not only did April and I want to get closer to our large families but also David Graham lived in Dallas and we knew we were not marketing ourselves adequately in his home state. We immediately settled into our new life with family, new friends, and a new church home; and our daughter, Shaylin, was born. We also signed several golf design jobs in the Dallas area. Once again, all was good.

In 1998, the partnership of Graham & Panks International ended, and I subsequently formed my own design company called The Linksmen. Starting a company this early in my career was not in original plans of life, but with past connections, I found quality design work. Also, owning my own company afforded me the ability to choose projects which would allow me to spend time with my growing family.

Golf course architecture is like most jobs. You take any work that comes your way, and you "grow, grow, grow." I was awarded membership to the American Society of Golf Course Architects and spent one week every year with other golf architects during our annual convention. I knew my travel schedule was difficult, but I kept hearing stories of architects from big firms constantly being away from family and multiple stories of divorces and kids being split between homes. That was very unappealing, as I wanted to be involved with my family. I wanted to coach Little League baseball and basketball and set up bounce houses for birthday parties. I wanted my kids to know their dad. I wanted to be involved at church and in the community. No amount of money and fame was worth losing relationships with my wife and family. Therefore, I decided I would stay a small design company and do only a select number of jobs rather than constantly on the road. I passed on a few design jobs that would have required travel and adding employees, but I was able to coach a lot of my children's teams. I know turning down some projects cost me a lot of money over the years and that contributed to some tough financial times ahead; but I see the relationships of our family, and I know I made the right choice.

In 1998, I had the great pleasure of joining forces with Phil Mickelson to design the Whisper Rock Golf Club in Scottsdale, Arizona. The developer was a gentleman named Gregg Tryhus, who was also the owner of the Grayhawk Golf Club (Talon Course) that I had designed in the early 1990s while with GPI. Gregg Tryhus is a remarkable man—successful, innovative, humble, generous, kind, and a true gentleman.

Gary Stephenson, Phil Mickelson, and Gregg Tryhus

Del Cochran was also instrumental in getting me and Phil together at Whisper Rock. Del was involved heavily at Grayhawk, and his ideas and fingerprints were widespread in the development. He always called me "Lad" and constantly described life as "a journey." I have used that term many times since the days in the desert at Grayhawk. Gregg and Del took a chance on me, and I will forever be in their debt.

Gregg and Del knew Phil from his early days at Arizona State University, and Phil visited Grayhawk during construction in the early 1990s. At the Grayhawk Grand Opening, Phil, his wife Amy, April, and I spent a good portion of the night at the same table, eating, talking, and listening to a private performance by Huey Lewis and the News. Phil had many exciting ideas about golf design, and that night, I knew he would be involved in the dirt somewhere. Little did I know his first foray into golf design was going to be five years later with me on a special project several miles north of where we were sitting that night.

The Whisper Rock Golf Club (Lower Course) in North Scottsdale was Phil's first ever design. In the planning and design phase, he and I spent a lot of time together, which was an immense pleasure. Phil is a very kind and generous person with a huge heart, especially for children. He is incredibly intelligent, interested in who you are and what you do, and is always probing your mind to learn and debate. He is quick with a joke and a masterful prankster. He is also humble.

One day during construction on the par 3, 12th hole, we were building a drop off on the back left of the green just off the collar. The decline was intended to be a gentle slope, but Phil wanted it to be more severe. He and I discussed it, and I said, "I didn't think it would look good if it was more severe, and I'm concerned about mowing it cleanly." One thing to understand is when Phil was on construction site visits, there was a larger crowd than when I would show up by myself. In addition to Phil and myself, there was the bulldozer operator (Tim), the construction superintendent (Steve) and his right-hand man (GJ), the golf course superintendent (Mike), Gregg Tryhus the owner, and a few other marketing and development team members. Everyone got involved in the conversation with no consensus being reached. We finally decided to have the shaper build the slope as Phil wanted, and we would come back in a few hours to review. After lunch, we came back to the 12th hole. Phil and I walked to the edge of the green and looked at it. Then we walked about fifteen yards behind the green and reviewed it from the edge of the desert. It was just the two of us by ourselves as the others knew to give us time for private discussion.

Phil turned to me with a slight smile of embarrassment on his face and whispered, "It really doesn't look very good, does it?"

I said, "Not really."

Phil then said, 'We shouldn't have changed it."

I replied, "Phil, this is how the process works. We make these modifications until we feel good about it, and then we call it 'good.'"

Phil then said, "I feel terrible about wasting everyone's time."

I replied, "Phil, you didn't waste anyone's time. This is how the process works."

Phil walked over to every person present and shook their hands and said, "I'm sorry I wasted your time. I should have left it alone."

They all said it was nothing to worry about and that the back-and-forth debate was great for the final outcome of the golf course. Many highly successful professional athletes are arrogant, rude, and condescending. That afternoon, I stood and watched the number 2 ranked player in the world apologize to every person because he thought he wasted a few minutes of their time. I have never forgotten that scene of humility and graciousness of Phil Mickelson.

Phil and I had many conversations and gentle debates throughout the design and construction of Whisper Rock. Phil had many wonderful ideas we incorporated into the design. We both wanted to think outside the box and do things never seen before, and it was rather amazing how we agreed on just about everything. Surprisingly, our biggest issue was getting everyone else comfortable with some radical ideas.

While Phil and I were working on Whisper Rock, I was also working on other projects in Georgia and Idaho. The Idaho project was a complete joy as I co designed that course with Byron Nelson and 1996 US Open Champion Steve Jones. This was just a few years before Mr. Nelson passed away, but his mind was incredibly sharp, and he was a true Christian gentleman. I was very blessed to be able to go to his ranch in the Dallas area and spend a few hours with him in his living room where he graciously answered all my questions about numerous tournaments and trophies. As we were both Christians, we also spent time talking faith and church. He was a great man, and I wish I would have been able to spend more time with him before his passing.

All of what happened next was overlapping in time. My family was living in McKinney, Texas, which is about thirty miles north of Dallas. We bought forty remote acres of land north of McKinney in a football-crazy town called Celina. I had always dreamed of owning land, and this spot was absolutely beautiful. I personally designed and helped build the house. At six bedrooms and over five thousand square feet, it was admittedly more than we needed. However, it was designed explicitly with the intent of our children and hopefully many future grandchildren to be able to visit in years to come. This was our dream house, and April and I intended to live there until our dying day.

Kids clearing trenches for water line to house.

The kids enjoyed the trips to the country during construction. They assisted in digging trenches for water and irrigation lines, helped to build the barbed wire fences around the old barn, and installed sod and landscaping. It was a full family effort.

It took over a year to build, but the day we moved into the ranch house was one of the happiest days of my life. I enjoyed living on the land more than words can express. I am reminded of the movie *Field of Dreams*. At the end, Ray Kinsella (Kevin Costner) is talking to his father who has come back to life with a group of ghostlike afterlife baseball players.

His father, John Kinsella (Dwier Brown), asks, Is this heaven?"

Ray answers, "It's Iowa."

His father says, "Could have sworn it was heaven."

Ray then asks, "Is...is there a heaven?"

John replies, "Oh yeah. It's the place dreams come true."

Ray then looks around the farm and then to his wife and daughter on the porch swing. He then says, "Maybe this is heaven."

There were times I would walk around the ranch and just marvel at the beauty and serenity of the place. On the land, I was at total and complete peace. I would watch April water the plants and the kids hit golf balls to our putting green or feed the longhorns. There were so many times I would think, *This must be heaven.* It was perfect.

It was during this time Phil Mickelson told me he wanted to start a golf design company and wanted me to work for him. His concept was intriguing. Instead of the usual designing multiple courses at a time, Phil wanted to only do one project at a time and make it the absolute best it could be. Once finished, we would move on to another project. We would only do very special, high-end projects in the most beautiful places in the world.

To me, it was a very interesting proposal. I would be working with Phil, which was very appealing. We would be working on some of the best projects in the world, which was also very appealing. However, as we would only be doing one project at a time, I would be making less money than doing multiple projects on my own; but the reduction in travel would allow more time with my family. That was the deciding factor; I wanted that family time.

Whisper Rock opened to rave reviews. I finished projects I was doing on my own, and then Phil and I joined forces in *Phil Mickelson Design*. As it turns out, the timing could not have been worse.

Getting extremely high-end golf design projects is difficult as those projects are very rare. I met with one man with an interesting project in Arizona, but we determined the permitting was going to be a nightmare, so we passed. Another developer had an utterly amazing piece of land on the coast in Mexico, but he could never get funding to materialize. I was getting frustrated, but Phil was reassuring. He said numerous times, "This is okay. We are only going to do the projects we want to do."

We started working with another group assembling a very nice project in the Dallas area. We created a development team with Del Cochran, who brought a high-end California-based hotelier to the project. The deal was to be finalized on a Thursday, but the Dallas developer had a funding delay and asked to push the meeting to finalize contracts and transfer funding to the following Tuesday. That meeting was rescheduled for 1:00 p.m. (CST) in Dallas, on Tuesday, September 11, 2001.

The first plane hit Tower 1 of the World Trade Center at 8:46 a.m. (EST). The second plane hit Tower 2 of the World Trade Center at 9:03 a.m. (EST). When I got to the 1:00 p.m. meeting, nobody had much interest in the project. We just sat in the conference room watching news of the terrorist attack. Around 1:30 p.m., the hotelier called and said, "There is no way we are building a hotel anywhere in the world until we find out what has happened today." The project ended that day, causing me to lose a design fee, a large commission for bringing the group together, and a fifteen-acre parcel within the development.

As mentioned earlier, the golf economy took a serious hit, and the high-end projects we were going after seemed to go away from 2001 to 2004. We tried to hang on for a while, but it didn't make sense for Phil to keep paying me for projects that weren't going to materialize, and I could potentially go after smaller projects and remodel work. So my working relationship with Phil ended. That was personally a very sad day as I truly enjoyed working with him.

It was during this time I began to turn to God in diligent prayer as I was seeing my life as the roller coaster. It was difficult to restart my design company from scratch, and the next couple of years was spent scrambling for any work at all. Finances got extremely tight. We spent all of our savings and started going deep into debt. Then, completely out of the blue, I got a call about an amazing remodel job on two courses in St. Andrews, Scotland. As the birthplace of golf, every golf architect dreams of working in St. Andrews.

I went further in debt buying the plane ticket to London, but this was an opportunity I could not miss. The developer put me up in the Savoy Hotel, which is one of the nicest hotels in London. I flew to Edinburg, Scotland, and drove to St. Andrews. After two days of review in St. Andrews, I spent one day back in London assembling my presentation. The owners planned to interview five golf architects over the next three weeks. The other four were the biggest names in all of golf and golf architecture. I was just representing "little ole me," and I was the first to interview. The presentation went very well, and I found the development team to be a group of very pleasant men dedicated to doing things right. As I finished, the owner asked me when I could start.

I asked, "Aren't you interviewing four other architects?"

He replied, "Not if you accept the job. We'll call them and tell them not to come."

Needless to say, the other architects got the call not to come. That night at dinner, I asked how they got my name in the first place since they were based in London and I was a lesser-known golf architect living in Texas. One of the men told me he called Gregg Tryhus and Del Cochran from Grayhawk and asked them for architect recommendations. As I mentioned earlier, I owe a lot to Gregg and Del.

Whisper Rock and the Fairmont St. Andrews Resort are two of my favorite golf courses to ever design. Whisper Rock was great because of the team and the vision Gregg Tryhus had for the course and development. Gregg has a knack for hiring people of the highest integrity and commitment, and these people lift his projects to great heights—men such as Trent Rathbun, the general manager of the club, a man of great knowledge, kindness, and sincerity.

Whisper Rock Golf Club in Scottsdale, Arizona.

The Fairmont St. Andrews in St. Andrews, Scotland.

St. Andrews was great because of the team—working with Johnny Robertson, Charles Head, Neil Ballingal, and Justin Wood of Fairmont Resort. While work was hard, we also took time to play golf throughout the country, and it was during a trip to a cold and windblown Elie Golf Club I witnessed Justin play the most amazing round of golf I have ever personally witnessed. The St. Andrews project was also wonderful due to the fact that English was spoken in this foreign country and that I was able to work in Scotland for three years allowing travel throughout the United Kingdom for sightseeing and golf. It was a thrill of a lifetime.

The design world began to heat up, and I got another project in the Dallas area and one in Austin. I was able to get back out of debt and once again set money aside for savings. In 2006, Phil Mickelson called and said there were potential projects in California, Mexico, and China he wanted me to help with. I had also gotten potential high-end projects for Phil and myself in Illinois and Idaho and a second project in the Austin area. The money I was going to make on those six projects alone was going to pay for all of our four kids' college educations and pay off the house and land.

However, as mentioned in the Preface, every one of those projects came to a halt when the economy crashed in September and October of 2008. The roller coaster immediately took another steep freefall.

I had always wanted April to be a stay-at-home mom to raise the children. Her constant presence and love with the children was extremely important to me. However, as funds tightened, she had to take a job with the Celina Independent School District as a teacher for special needs children. It was very painful seeing her leave the house every day, but she never once complained. We prayed constantly for God's help and guidance.

While all of this was happening, April's mother had been diagnosed with bladder cancer in December 2007. Living in Duncan, Oklahoma, she fought the cancer for a year, and it appeared to be in remission. Then in 2009, her cancer returned with a vengeance, and everyone knew it was going to be a difficult journey. Cancer is not a fair fight, and we prayed.

In 2010, our financial situation had gotten severe. We cut our budget down to absolute essentials. We had to sell our barn and thirty of our forty acres, and we sold the cattle. We cut out our large garden because we couldn't afford the water bill. Life was hard, and we prayed.

In the late summer of 2010, I got a call from Phil Mickelson's agent, Steve Loy, saying the China project was back on and they wanted me to run the project. The job required me to move to Kunming, China, for eighteen months, with four two-week return visits during that time. The proposed salary was very good, and I would have all expenses paid, including a house and driver. In our financial situation, I would have normally jumped at the opportunity without hesitation. But this was a different time. I spoke with April and the kids, and we all prayed diligently about this difficult decision. Garrett would be going to college in the fall, but there would still be three children at home whom April would be responsible for. I knew April would need to travel to Oklahoma to visit her mother.

In addition to financial need, I knew turning this project down meant I would likely never work with Phil ever again. The decision was agonizing, yet obvious; I simply could not go to China and leave April in Texas with the kids while her mother was dying of cancer.

In a show of loving support, several fellow teachers at Celina Middle School pooled their vacation days together and gave them to April to spend additional time with her mother and father. Thankfully, April spent the last thirty-five days of her mother's life with her. On Wednesday, December 15, 2010, Virginia Bryant "won" her battle against cancer and went to be with "her Jesus." She was a source of boundless joy and love and had a soul-deep passion for the Lord. While the heavenly choir improved that day, her passing was an excruciating blow to the family. I will never forget, after April informed me of the news, I called Jacob, Brooks, and Shaylin together and painfully told them of Nana's passing. April called Garrett at Oklahoma Christian University to tell him; he was studying for finals. We all cried and prayed.

Baby Garrett, April, and Virginia Bryant (1991)

Christmas of 2010 was very emotional as it was the first Christmas without Nana, and we had no money for gifts or a traditional Christmas meal. Instead of the customary large Christmas, April and I got no gifts for each other; and the kids each got a package of underwear, a package of socks, and a package of gum. Not once did the kids ever complain.

2011 was amazingly hard. I continued to look for any work possible. We were dead broke. We knew we were likely to lose the house and remaining land. We worked with the mortgage company to refinance. Every month we sent fifty to sixty pages of tax returns, bank statements, and income verification, but could never get a final answer from them regarding refinancing. What would we do if we lost the house? We prayed diligently asking God to help.

I was personally worn down and beaten as the overwhelming stress was wrecking my body physically. I was watching my family sink into this financial abyss, and the impact was hard on them as well. Around-the-clock, nonstop calls from credit card companies and banks were maddening, and we eventually simply unplugged the phones. I woke every morning not knowing what to do. I had called everyone I knew, but there was no work. I was useless. I was failing my family. I had lost my identity, as I was no longer a golf course architect. Embarrassed and humiliated, I was terrified as I felt the onset of a nervous breakdown and depression. I was spiritually crushed and prayed for God to help me avoid the mental abyss.

In addition to the personal feelings of failure, I was dealing with anger and hatred. When the collapse began in September 2008, I had significant invoices out to clients. Some invoices were at the thirty-day period of being due, and a new batch of invoices was just being sent out. One project in particular was being billed a very large sum of money as we had just completed a significant milestone in the design fee. When the financial collapse happened, several of the companies we were working for filed for bankruptcy. Others tried to hang on but were cash-strapped and told me they had larger monetary obligations they were addressing before they could deal with my design fee. As a result, I was not paid on invoices totaling more than $505,000. When you are in severe financial distress and you are seeing the effects it has on your family, there is an anger that builds toward the people who owe you money.

Anger. Anger. Anger. If allowed to build, this anger can become an all-consuming raging fire that can easily destroy an already weakened soul. It is like a stage 4 cancer that grows and forces out any measure of love and compassion within the heart. Anger is a wonderfully effective tool of Satan.

In mid-2011, April began feeling ill. She finally went to the doctor and was told she might have cancer. After losing her mother to cancer the previous December, this was extremely difficult to hear and obviously scared us all. If April had cancer, we had to keep her job because our insurance was through her work. But, if we lost the house, would we be able to stay in Celina for her job? What would we do if we were homeless and she had cancer?

Our middle son, Jacob, had joined Garrett at Oklahoma Christian University; so it was just April and me at home with Brooks and Shaylin. On Monday, November 14, April went in for exploratory surgery. April's father and sister sat with me in the waiting room. The day was tense and long. Late that night, we were informed the lab reports had come back negative; April did not have cancer. Many prayers were answered, and tears of joy flowed that night.

The next morning, Tuesday, November 15, a certified letter from our mortgage company was hand delivered to inform us of the starting of the foreclosure process. We called and talked to a new lady at the mortgage company because our representative was no longer there. We explained we had been trying to refinance for over six months and had done all they requested. She told us that even though we had been filling out what they requested, it was the wrong paperwork and was useless. We repeatedly asked, "If we were filling out everything you sent to us, why was it the wrong paperwork?" We spent a long time on the phone with her, but she was cold and uncaring and would not budge. She let us know we would likely have to leave the house by early February. This was a devastating blow that crushed the joy of the negative cancer results the night before. April and I cried many tears of sorrow that night. And we prayed.

With no money, we knew we had to go somewhere we could live for free. We called my middle brother in Lubbock, Texas, and they said we could live with them. We had not talked to Brooks or Shaylin about moving because we had been trying to develop a plan depending on the cancer results. We were then informed that if the kids wanted to play spring sports, they must be enrolled in Lubbock by December 7. They both played basketball, baseball, and softball so they needed to be enrolled. So, during Thanksgiving break, we announced we were moving to Lubbock on December 6. They only had ten days' notice that they were leaving everything they knew and loved—friends, school, church, family, and our home. Many tears of sadness were cried that night from everyone in the house. There was not much thanksgiving.

On the night of December 6, I took the kids to Lubbock, while April stayed to finish the school semester and to start packing the house. At Christmas break, Brooks, Shay, and I drove back to Celina and joined Garrett and Jacob who had returned home from college. Packing up the house was very difficult, especially at Christmas time. There was no money for a tree or gifts. The boys found a small evergreen tree from one of the pastures and put it on a small ladder in the living room, which generated a much-needed laugh. One of April's teacher friends gave her some Walmart gift cards for Christmas, for which we were eternally thankful as we purchased food and got each one of the kids a pair of blue jeans and a few other essentials.

As we were moving from a five thousand-square-foot house to live with my brother's family, we had to throw away, sell, or donate a lot of furniture, many household items, tools, and clothes. Each item put into a box, or tossed into the dumpster or bonfire, felt like we were destroying memories. Finally, on December 31, we loaded everything up and pulled four cars and a small moving van out of the long driveway.

This was going to be the last time I would ever close and lock the gate at the entrance of the beloved land. I was in the lead car, and after we all pulled through the gate, I stopped to shut the gate. This required walking by each of the other cars in the caravan. Making my way to the gate, I looked at the faces of April and my children. Try as they might, their overwhelming pain and sorrow was impossible to hide. I felt like ten tons of bricks were crashing down on me. Several times on this walk I felt like my knees were going to give out on me and I would fall to the ground. I had completely failed my family and caused immense sadness. That was unquestionably the hardest single day of my life. To the deepest depth of my soul, I was completely saddened, humbled, and broken.

To be honest, what bothered me most was that age-old question of "Why do bad things happen to good people?" We were trying to live to glorify God. We tried to be kind and generous. We were active in church and the community. And yet, we were dealing with death, sickness, and losing everything. This seemed so unfair and undeserved.

Several years have passed since locking the gate, and our financial difficulties have been severe and ongoing. The golf economy has never recovered, and my very specialized resume doesn't seem to travel. The journey has been hard and extremely discouraging. I still don't understand all of our hard times and difficulties. When we lost the house and land, we lost things, but the picture of those hurt faces in the cars is burned deep into my mind. I still struggle with the hurt of that moment, and I pray diligently for God to help erase that memory and profound pain.

During these trials and tribulations, my prayer life and Bible study had been a roller coaster. However, one day of study introduced me to Psalm 73 and a man named Asaph. I immediately related to him because he was complaining about having struggles while the arrogant and wicked were prosperous and mocking God. "Pride is their necklace."[2] Asaph was laying out a list of objections. Then he made a turn in his thinking. In verse 21, Asaph said:

> When my heart was grieved and my spirit embittered, I was senseless and ignorant; I was a brute beast before you. Yet I am always with you; you hold me by my right hand. You guide me with your counsel, and afterward you will take me to glory. Whom have I in heaven but you? And earth has nothing I desire besides you. My flesh and my heart may fail, but God is the strength of my heart and my portion forever.[3]

---

[2] Psalm 73:6
[3] Psalm 73:21–26

As I read the line "…earth has nothing I desire besides you," I wonder if Asaph would include a house, forty acres of land, and cattle—things of earth.

I know, in the whole scheme of life and the world, our difficulties pale in comparison to what other people face every day. We have clean water and clothes. We have our health. We have a strong family and good friends. We have love. And most importantly, we have a heavenly Father who loves us and desires us to walk with him. Even so, it is hard to walk when you are broken and limping. It is hard when things don't make sense.

In the writings of Paul, I encounter God's ability to use us in our weakness and even when we have a "thorn in the flesh." It is never revealed what Paul's thorn is, but he pleaded three times for the Lord to remove it:

> To keep me from becoming conceited because of these surpassingly great revelations, there was given me a thorn in my flesh, a messenger of Satan, to torment me. But he said to me, "My grace is sufficient for you, for my power is made perfect in weakness." Therefore I will boast all the more gladly about my weaknesses, so that Christ's power may rest on me. That is why, for Christ's sake, I delight in weaknesses, in insults, in hardships, in persecutions, in difficulties. For when I am weak, then I am strong.[4]

I don't know why God never took his thorn away. Paul seemed to think it was to keep him humble and to concentrate on God. Paul decided to turn it into a source of strength.

Do you struggle with a thorn in your life? Do you know what your thorn is? Can you identify it? I can. The thorn in my flesh is the hurt on the faces of my children and wife the day I closed the gate. Satan knows any time he wants me to be angry or disappointed with

---

[4] 2 Corinthians 12:7–10

God, he simply flashes that memory to the forefront of my mind. Like a red-hot branding iron, the pain is still searing. You would think it would be easy to remove the thorn when you know what it is. It isn't. It is a constant struggle I take to God.

Do you have something in your life that causes pain and suffering? Do you have memories that haunt you? Maybe memories of mistakes or decisions and actions in life you wish you could go back and change?

What did Paul's thorn generate? Was it physical discomfort? Was it spiritual despair? We don't know. We simply know he asked the Lord to take it away. Three times, the Lord's reply was, no, "My grace is sufficient for you, for my power is made perfect in your weakness."[5]

On top of the sorrowful loss of Nana and financial stress, the thorn in my flesh is the byproduct of the loss of our land and home—the loss of things. I mentioned earlier the land and home was my dream. But I look back and wonder, *Was it God's dream for me?* I have thought deeply about this; but, before we bought the land and built that large home, I don't remember ever laying it all out before God and asking if this was his will or if he would bless our efforts. I simply moved forward and built our "heaven on earth." I am reminded Jesus said, "For where your treasure is, there your heart will be also."[6] The land and home was definitely my treasure; that was where my heart was. It was not on worshiping and obeying God.

I said Satan has the ability to make me angry at God. Why? Over what? The loss of things. The loss of material possessions. Embarrassment. Failure. Like the *Seinfeld*-based tradition of Festivus, I have tried to imagine angrily confronting God with my "Festivus list of grievances" toward him.

"God, I am angry at you for taking away my things." (As I type those words, I am struck by how childish that sounds.)

I can almost hear God's reply, "Did you say 'your things'? Hmm, that's interesting. Well, Gary…while you're listing your complaints about

---

[5] 1 Corinthians 12:9
[6] Matthew 6:21

me, don't let the fact you have a wife and children who love you cloud your mind. And certainly avoid the fact your sons have married godly women, because I was listening all those nights when they were young when you and April prayed about that. Oh, along those lines of your growing family, I've been meaning to apologize that you had to get the extra chairs out of garage storage because there were too many people at your dinner table last Christmas. I'm sure that was a hassle. But let's get back to your list… Make sure you skip over the blessings of your extended earthly family who has been there for you at every turn; that must get old thanking them for their prayers and financial help. Oh, and the same goes for your earthly spiritual family and friends.

Since you're on a roll, don't let those pictures on your walls of all the beautiful places you've worked around the world distract you or make your mind wander; stay focused on your list of grievances.

I know your upset about Nana leaving you all. I would ask her to let you know it's okay, but I can't get her to quit laughing and dancing and singing long enough to tell you. And speaking of heavenly beings, I recommend you not mention all the countless times your guardian angels have protected you from danger; but, since you don't know about those, just forget I brought that up.

And, Gary, while you're at it, don't let that cross hanging down from your neck block the view of the keyboard you're hammering away at. By the way, why are you wearing that necklace?"

He pauses to let me think. Like the Jewish leaders dropping the jagged stones they intended to throw at the woman caught in adultery,[7] my enthusiasm to finish my list of grievances wanes. God's voice changes. The laughing glint of gentle sarcasm is gone, replaced by an amazing calm and compassion.

"I know you were hurt and the journey has been hard. You have a thorn in your flesh because you lost things. My son wore a crown of thorns on his head, and he lost his life so that you would have more than you 'can ever ask or imagine.[8] I love you and your family more than you will ever understand love can be. My grace is sufficient. If you will allow me

---

[7] John 8:3–11

[8] Ephesians 3:20

to, I can do great things in your weakness, and you will experience divine joy beyond measure. Let go of the pain of the past, and let's build new dreams. But let's do them together."

I know I am broken and weary. I know Satan has done a masterful job of diverting my mind from the divine to the human and exploiting pride, envy, and apathy. I know I must seek contentment and healing. But I am also certain God's idea of healing will differ from mine.

In hopeful humility, I ask God, "Can you work with someone like me who is bruised and battered and drowning in the waves?"

The booming joy returns to his voice as he proclaims, "I do my best work in the middle of storms."

My thorn ♦ Paul's thorn ♦ Jesus's thorns

Chapter 3

A Small Word

"How did this happen?"

My office was on the second floor of our house. I specifically designed my office so I could stand at different windows and on the balcony and see almost all of the forty acres. Time was drawing near to losing the home to the mortgage company. We sold the cattle, and to make ends meet, we sold thirty acres of the land, including the barn. It is amazing how your mind falls in love with particular scenes. The barn at sunset was beautiful, and the longhorn cattle were the finishing touch on the Norman Rockwell painting. When the longhorns were gone, the land looked empty.

We still owned the land where the vegetable garden was located, but we abandoned it when we could no longer afford the water bill. Losing the garden was hard. Not only did we not have fresh vegetables for our table but also one of our ministries was taking buckets of vegetables each week to the food pantry at church. The other thing I missed was feeding the longhorns their beloved watermelon and cantaloupe. Every time I worked in the garden, the longhorns lined the fence almost begging me to throw watermelon and cantaloupe into their pasture. They looked like kids in line at an ice-cream truck. The big bull dominated the food, so I spread everything out in hopes the cows and yearlings could get some before the bull would effortlessly move them away with a purposeful nudge of his thick powerful horns.

One morning, I stood at a window looking toward the barn and pasture. It looked so hollow. There were no cows or horses, just empty stalls and corrals. Even though the garden was dried up, there were still two dozen metal tomato hoops standing upright. But they were nothing more than rusting sentinels proclaiming emptiness. Faded cornstalk stubbles revealed old rows dug by hand. It was demoralizing.

Each morning, I tried studying the Bible. But lately, my study was erratically unfocused. I was searching and discouraged. I had gotten to the point where I would randomly open my Bible and look for question marks. When found, I would read and consider the question. Then I would read before and after the question to see what it was about and how it had been addressed. It was interesting at times, but scattershooting at best. I was trying to stay in the Word, but was fighting disinterest and increasing doubt. I was lonely and lost. My Bible study devolved into aimlessly opening my Bible and reading wherever chance dictated.

This morning, alone in the large house, I looked out the window for a long time. April was at work and the kids at school. The emptiness and loss seemed magnified as I kept asking myself, "How did this happen? Why?"

I walked to my desk and opened the Bible, hoping for something uplifting and encouraging, maybe a psalm about deliverance, maybe something about blessings and victory. The Bible opened with a gentle thud, and I was not overjoyed when I saw the "Habakkuk" heading at the top of the page. I thought, *You've got to be kidding me. Habakkuk?* Another punch in the gut.

The top left of the page started at chapter 2, verse 10. "…shaming your house and forfeiting your life. The stones of the wall will cry out, and the beams of the woodwork will echo it." Sarcastically, I thought, *Hey, that's encouraging.*

I kept reading, and verses 18–20 began to create some pause:

> Of what value is an idol, since man has carved it? Or an image that teaches lies? For he who makes it trusts in his own creation; he makes idols that cannot speak. Woe to him who says to wood, "Come to life!" Or to lifeless stone, "Wake up!" Can it give guidance? It is covered with gold and silver; there is no breath in it. But the Lord is in his Holy temple; let all the earth keep silent before him.[9]

I was definitely familiar with the last line, recognizing it as one of my favorite church songs that I remembered my mom singing when I was a young boy. I had never known that soul-stirring song is from Habakkuk. While that was comforting, the other verses about man-made idols and trusting in your own creation struck an uncomfortable chord. "Can a house and a forty-acre ranch be an idol? Certainly not."

I kept reading. The heading for chapter 3 is "Habakkuk's Prayer":

> Lord, I have heard of your fame;…(verse 2)
> Plague went before him:…(verse 5)
> Sun and moon stood still in the heavens…
> (verse 11)

---

[9] Habakkuk 2:18–20

I heard and my heart pounded,...(verse 16)

Though the fig tree does not bud and there are no grapes on the vines, though the olive crop fails and the fields produce no food, though there are no sheep I the pen and no cattle in the stalls,...(verse 17)

I literally stopped reading at this point. I asked, "What am I reading? A failed garden? No cattle in the stalls?" This quickly got personal and uncomfortable. I turned and looked toward the window where I had just been standing while gazing at the land. I read this passage again:

> Though the fig tree does not bud and there are no grapes on the vines, though the olive crop fails and the fields produce no food, though there are no sheep in the pen and no cattle in the stalls, yet I will rejoice in the LORD, I will be joyful in God my Savior. The Sovereign LORD is my strength; he makes my feet like the feet of a deer, he enables me to go on the heights.[10]

Have you ever had a passage speak to you personally?

I had literally just stood at the window seeing the exact images of what I just read. How did I entirely by chance open my Bible to this passage? Habakkuk? Was it chance that out of 2,105 total pages in my *NIV Study Bible* I opened the book to pages 1,390–1,391 which described the exact scene I was looking at a few minutes earlier? Do I dare ask, "Did God somehow make me turn to this passage?" That's absurd, right? These are the kinds of things you don't ever talk about away from church folks because everyone will laugh at you. Even some church people will snicker if you suggest God opened your Bible to a specific spot. Does God even work that way?

---

[10] Habakkuk 3:17–19

I reread verses 17–19 at least a half dozen times. I looked at the study notes at the bottom of the page:

> Habakkuk has learned the lesson of faith (2:4)—
> to trust in God's providence regardless of circum-
> stances. He declares that even if God should send
> suffering and loss, he would still rejoice in his
> Savior-God—one of the strongest affirmations
> of faith in all Scripture.[11]

Habakkuk was describing the exact experiences of my life, but he spoke of rejoicing while I was sinking in complete despair and sadness. His prayer was victory and rejoicing; mine was defeat and sorrow. Here is the dangerous aspect of this: we can look at someone else's strength in dealing with adversity compared to our despair, and it discourages us even further because you see yourself weaker and less of a believer than the one who is strong and full of faith. It is a very slippery slope that Satan loves to push us toward.

Have you ever been there? Have you ever experienced not knowing how to pray or what to pray for? A place where you're all prayed out? A place where you are fearful of what is around the corner?

For the next few days, I couldn't get Habakkuk out of my mind. There was a familiarity to it I couldn't shake. "…yet I will rejoice…"

I found myself wondering how I could find strength and calm through prayer. I read about prayers of thanksgiving, joy, despair, sorrow, courage, faith, hope, and so on. I spent time in the Psalms and then looked at the prayers of Christ, especially the prayers in the Garden of Gethsemane. In the garden, Jesus was at the end of so many things—his life on earth, his time with beloved friends and disciples, his ministry. We see Jesus in complete despair telling his disciples, "My soul is overwhelmed with sorrow to the point of death…"[12] His depth of despair is described even further as Luke

---

[11] *NIV Study Bible*, page 1,391
[12] Matthew 26:38

records, "And being in anguish, he prayed more earnestly, and his sweat was like drops of blood falling to the ground."[13]

Jesus left Peter and the two sons of Zebedee (James and John) and went off to pray by himself. "Going a little farther, he fell with his face to the ground and prayed. 'My Father, if it is possible, may this cup be taken from me....'"[14]

This prayer is amazing. Jesus is the Son of God. He came to the earth to be a sacrifice. He literally left his place in heaven and dwelt among men for the events of this very night. And still, he was so overcome with grief and sorrow that he asked if there was another way to accomplish the goal.

Is it strange that I find comfort in that? Pardon my irreverence, but isn't Jesus saying, "I'm not excited about the road you have me going down, Dad. I'm not diggin' this plan"? I see myself in that; I relate! I see the times when I am facedown in total defeat and strength-sapping despair and asking God to please pull me out of the "mud and mire."[15]

Then I read on:

> Going a little farther, he fell with his face to the ground and prayed, "My Father, if it is possible, may this cup be taken from me. Yet not as I will, but thine be done."[16]

"...Yet not as I will, but thine be done." A complete reversal in attitude. "God, I do not like this plan, but if this is your will, I will do it." Completer surrender. Complete obedience. Complete trust.

And do you know what I find most amazing about this? This entire dichotomy hinges on one small word, "yet." There is a conflict of eternally epic proportions occurring here, and the word "yet" is the linchpin it all turns on.

---

[13] Luke 22:44
[14] Matthew 26:39
[15] Psalm 40:2
[16] Matthew 26:39

As I sat at my desk and read, there was a strange familiarity to Jesus's prayer in the garden. I then looked to the window and remembered my looking at the land and reading of Habakkuk. I went back and forth between Habakkuk and the Gospel of Matthew, and the familiarity became obvious—a small word…"yet."

> Though the fig tree does not bud and there are no grapes on the vines, though the olive crop fails and the field produces no food, though there are no sheep in the pen and no cattle in the stalls, *yet* I will rejoice in the Lord, I will be joyful in God my Savior. The Sovereign Lord is my strength; he makes my feet like the feet of a deer, he enables me to go on the heights. (Habakkuk 3:17–19)

Habakkuk was lamenting the emptiness and loss. "Yet" he proclaimed that he would not concentrate on those things, but would instead rejoice in the Lord.

Dictionary.com defines the word "yet" as "though the case be such; nevertheless." How do these two passages read with this definition inserted?

> Though the fig tree does not bud and there are no grapes on the vines, though the olive crop fails and the field produces no food, though there are no sheep in the pen and no cattle in the stalls, (though the case be such; nevertheless) I will rejoice in the Lord, I will be joyful in God my Savior. The Sovereign Lord is my strength; he makes my feet like the feet of a deer, he enables me to go on the heights.[17]
>
> Going a little farther, he fell with his face to the ground and prayed, "My Father, if it is possible, may this cup be taken from me. (Though

---

[17] Habakkuk 3:17–19

the case be such; nevertheless) not as I will, but thine be done."[18]

In both instances, it is a change of attitudes and priorities born out of complete trust. Habakkuk was looking at the loss, but he trusted that God would give him strength and lift him to new heights. Jesus was about to face a horrifically painful and humiliating death, but he trusted God and completely surrendered to his will. He was wholly obedient to his Father.

Unfortunately, we tend to sing "Trust and Obey" as just a children's song, but the depth of that song is beyond measure in the fact that true obedience is based wholly on trust. You will not release control of material things to someone unless you trust them. You will not release control of your life to someone unless you wholly trust them. Trust and obedience cannot be separated.

Dictionary.com defines "obedience" as "the act or practice of obeying; dutiful or submissive compliance. A sphere of authority or jurisdiction, especially ecclesiastical." I choose to define it as "acting on the realization that someone knows better than you do what is best for you."

In the summer of 2017, I had surgery to repair a previous hernia surgery performed many years earlier. The surgery went fine and recovery on schedule. However, two weeks after the surgery, the incision got infected. On a Sunday morning, I went to my brother's house for him to observe the incision. He is an orthopedic surgeon and told me I needed to be in the hospital on antibiotics. I told him I couldn't go to the hospital because I had to be in San Marcos for a meeting the next morning as four guys were flying in from Phoenix and Houston to meet with me on a golf construction site. My wife and I were in financial difficulty, and I could not risk doing anything to put the job in jeopardy. So, that evening, I drove six very uncomfortable hours from Lubbock to San Marcos. The next day was long, hot, and very painful. When I got to the hotel, I texted pictures of my stomach to my brother, and he recommended I go to an ER. Once again, I told

---

[18] Matthew 26:39

him I couldn't afford the cost and would try to get home to Lubbock the next day where he could help me. After several hours, the increasing pain forced me to go to the walk-in ER. Around 11:00 p.m., I checked in and went to "Room 1." The doctor took one look at my stomach and immediately ordered an IV antibiotic "soup," blood work, and a CT scan. The nurse inserted a large number 22 needle that I later found out is referred to as "a fire hydrant," because it is trying to get antibiotics into the bloodstream very quickly. As she worked, she looked at me and said, "You have no idea how sick you are." The results of the scan showed an abscess the size of a baseball just below the incision. The doctor recommended surgery immediately. All I saw was dollar signs. I told him, "If I can just get back to Lubbock tomorrow, I will be okay." He kept trying to persuade me of the need for surgery and even called my brother to have him confirm the need for surgery, which he did. I kept saying, "I can't."

Finally, the doctor pulled a chair up next to my bed and said, "If this infection travels down to your hernia mesh, you will be fighting this infection for months. If it breaks through your abdominal wall, you will go septic and likely die." He was serious. He was no longer smiling or mild mannered. His voice and tone had changed. At that point, I accepted the realization that he knew better than I did what was best for me. I said I would have the surgery. He said he would call for an ambulance to take me to the hospital. Again, I said I couldn't afford it and I'd just drive there myself. He looked at me and firmly said, "You are going to die." I went to the hospital in the ambulance. The surgery was successful. My wife traveled down and was able to get me back to Lubbock.

I look back in embarrassment by the number of times I said, "I can't." I ignored advice of experts and only considered limitations of money. It was not a time of courage, trust, and obedience, but rather a defeatist attitude of excuses that introduced the possibility of death.

I compare my defeatist attitude with the courage of Christ in the Garden of Gethsemane. Jesus knew what death by crucifixion meant. He knew the indescribable torture that awaited him. He was in complete anguish, yet he approached it with unabridged trust and obedience. The firm foundation of trust and obedience was the fact that he knew God the Father. Their relationship was so deep and intimate that Jesus knew God is faithful, true, just, loving, and merciful and he keeps his promises. Jesus knew that if something was God's desire, it was worthy and noble. That trust led Jesus to the cross and, three days later, out of the grave.

Obedience is based on faith and trust in God when things don't seem to make sense.

- A humble Moses approaching the throne of Pharaoh telling him to let God's people go[19]
- An innocent Joseph when he was repeatedly thrown into pits[20]
- Joshua walking around Jericho seven times[21]
- Queen Esther putting on her makeup as she was about to face her husband king uninvited[22]
- Job as he used a piece of broken pottery to scrape painful sores on his body[23]
- Daniel sleeping peacefully in the middle of a den of hungry lions[24]
- Shadrach, Meshach, and Abednego when things got warm in the fiery furnace[25]
- Stephen as the angry stones flew[26]
- Paul and Silas singing in their dark prison cell[27]

All were in situations where severe pain and possible death was a likely outcome. How did they overcome fear and lean on faith and

---

[19] Exodus 3–12
[20] Genesis 37:23–24, Genesis 39:20
[21] Joshua 6
[22] Esther 4:12–16
[23] Job 2:7–8
[24] Daniel 6
[25] Daniel 3
[26] Acts 7:54–60
[27] Acts 16:22–30

courage? Trust and obedience born of the belief that God knows better than I do what is best for me.

Why is trust and obedience so difficult? I believe there are two reasons for our struggles. First, "The trials and tribulations we face often make no sense." In my mind, logic should rule everything. I am a designer by trade, and I think of life the same way. Because everything must fit within reason, I draw a line on a page to create an evident and clear plan. But life is not always evident and clear and is often full of things that make no sense. We find frustration and doubt while searching for human reason.

Second, "Why does it need to take so long?" We want things done now. We want quick resolution to difficulties in life. It is so hard to understand the concept of time and eternity, because our minds are limited by clocks and calendars. God's is not. We view all aspects of our lives in terms of hours, days, weeks, months, and years. God's view is through the lens of eternity. I look at my circumstances, and I say, "I must do something now to get out of this bad situation." God says, "Trust me. I've got something great in store for you if you will just weather this storm with me."

We want a resolution written on this year's calendar. God says, "Trust me. I have a plan."

- At age seventy-five, Abraham was promised a child, and he wanted it in nine months. God said, "Let's wait twenty-five years, so there is no doubt it was because of me that Isaac was born." Abraham remained faithful, and God used Isaac to bless an entire nation.
- Joseph had been thrown in a pit by his brothers and sold to a traveling caravan. He then was thrown into prison due to false claims against him. For years he languished in prison. Then, he interpreted a dream that helped the cupbearer be released. Joseph thought the cupbearer would help him get a quick release as well. But the cupbearer forgot about him, and it took two more years for Joseph to find freedom. Through years of pain and disappointment, Joseph remained faithful, and God eventually moved him into a

position of power to save his family and the entire Israelite people.

- Moses spent the first forty years of his life in Egyptian glamour, followed by forty years in the desert experiencing humility and nothingness. Then, he spent the last forty years of his life babysitting two million ungrateful Israelites. Moses remained faithful and was taken to a mountaintop where he got to look into the promised land, the place prepared by God for his people.

- Joshua and Caleb were two of the twelve spies sent into Canaan. They came back with a positive report and said, "With God, we can take it." But, due to the weak faith of the ten other spies and the Israelite people, Joshua and Caleb had to wander in the wilderness for forty more years while they watched unbelievers, their friends, die by the wayside. They remained faithful and finally got to cross the Jordan River and inhabit the place of promise, and Caleb got his mountain.

The examples can go on and on. It doesn't make sense, and it takes so long. And all the while, God is saying, "Trust me. I know better than you do what is best for you."

Another important aspect to remember is "my life does not just affect me." Abraham had to wait twenty-five years to have a son who blessed an entire nation. Joseph experienced years of misery to finally be in a position of power to help his family and the entire Israelite people.

Is my life, is your life, being set up to somehow bless other people in the future?

Are you set on a course designed by God that will bless people you don't even know?

Do we have these diversions, detours, and pitfalls so that God can get us into a different position and use us to fulfill his will in an area we can't begin to anticipate?

I don't know. Whether our lives are being used to bless others or we are simply on trajectories to develop stronger personal relationships with God, I pray we will be like Habakkuk and rejoice and trust and obey. I pray we will remember the power of the word "yet."

I think of the examples of people persevering with faith while in trial and tribulation. I think of how their "yet's" have impacted the lives of millions, or even billions, of people throughout history—most importantly, Jesus's amazing proclamation of "…yet, not my will but thine…" and the subsequent hope of salvation that produced.

There is another "yet" that has led to a multitude of lives in Christ. Three days after the crucifixion, unbeknownst to the disciples and his friends and followers, Jesus had risen from death. Mary Magdalene and the other Mary went to anoint Jesus's dead body. Matthew 28 reads:

> After the Sabbath, at dawn on the first day of the week, Mary Magdalene and the other Mary went to look at the tomb.
>
> There was a violent earthquake, for an angel of the Lord came down from heaven and, going to the tomb, rolled back the stone and sat on it. His appearance was like lightning, and his clothes were as white as snow. The guards were so afraid of him that they shook and became like dead men.
>
> The angel said to the women, "Do not be afraid, for I know that you are looking for Jesus, who was crucified. He is not here; he is risen, just as he said. Come and see the place where he lay. Then go quickly and tell his disciples: 'He has risen from the dead and is going ahead of you into Galilee. There you will see him. Now I have told you.'"
>
> So the women hurried away from the tomb, afraid *yet* filled with joy, and ran to tell his disciples.[28]

---

[28] Matthew 28:1–8 (NIV)

I love that last line: "afraid *yet* filled with joy." The rest is his-story.

I pray that you and I will overcome fear and disappointment in life. I pray we will experience...the power of a small word...yet.

> In this you greatly rejoice, though now for a little while, if need be, you have been grieved by various trials, that the genuineness of your faith, being much more precious than gold that perishes, though it is tested by fire, may be found to praise, honor, and glory at the revelation of Jesus Christ, whom you have not seen you love. Though now you do not see Him, *yet* believing, you rejoice with joy inexpressible and full of glory, receiving the end of your faith—the salvation of your souls. (1 Peter 1:8–9 NKJV)

> I have been deprived of peace; I have forgotten what prosperity is. So I say, "My splendor is gone and all that I had hoped from the LORD." I remember my affliction and my wandering, the bitterness and the gall. I well remember them, and my soul is downcast within me. *Yet* this I call to mind and therefore I have hope: Because of the LORD's great love we are not consumed, for his compassion never fails. They are new every morning; great is your faithfulness. I say to myself, "The LORD is my portion; therefore I will wait for him." The LORD is good to those whose hope is in him, to the one who seeks him; it is good to wait quietly for the salvation of the LORD. (Lamentations 3:17–26 NIV)

Chapter 4

Alone

Alone.

I only saw him for a total of five or six seconds; but that was enough. It was August of 2015, the start of a new school year, and I was driving past an elementary school in our neighborhood. It was recess time, and kids were all over the playground. Some kids were on the swing sets and monkey bars. Others were playing soccer or throwing a football. Some kids were standing together in groups just talking; and yes, these were mainly girls. Teachers were huddled together in the shade of the school building watching the children and no doubt talking about the start of the new school year. Everyone was together. Everyone was active. Everyone seemed to be enjoying the sunny day.

Except for him. He was alone.

He stood alone under this tall tree.

Standing by himself in the shade under a large tree, he was watching a nearby group of boys playing soccer. Even though he appeared to be healthy and "normal," he looked different from the other kids on the playground. Most of the kids were wearing shorts, tee shirts, and tennis shoes. He was wearing a brown and tan plaid button-up short-sleeved shirt tucked into neatly pressed blue jeans that appeared to be part of his new school clothes. It was hard to see, but it looked like he was wearing a kind of casual brown dress shoes. His brown hair was neatly combed and parted on the right side of his head.

Alone.

When I saw him, I wondered if he was new to the school and didn't know anyone yet. The way he was dressed made me wonder if he was living with his grandparents and if it was his grandmother who had dressed him this way and combed his hair for school. His look was vintage.

I immediately began to ask myself questions about this young boy:

- What kind of family did he come from?
- Was he a nice boy? Shy and quiet?
- Was he mean and nobody wanted to be around him?
- Did he have low self-esteem?
- Was he socially awkward?
- Or was he just "the new kid" and his chance would eventually come?

Alone.

His eyes were set on the boys playing soccer. His hands were together just above his belt, and the way his fingers were fidgeting, they spoke of a desire to be in the game. I imagined he desperately wanted to run in, take the ball, and score a quick goal. He wanted to be running and playing and sweating and messing up his neatly combed hair. "Was he a good soccer player?" "Would he impress the other boys if he got to play?" "Did he have the courage to enter the fray, or was he destined to stand on the sideline in the shade under the tree...alone?"

Have you ever been alone?

I know there are times when you want to be alone, times when you just need to get away and rest and relax for a little while and catch your breath. But have you ever been alone when you didn't want to be? I am an introvert. Being alone doesn't really bother me. When April and I are invited to a party or gathering of some sort, I am perfectly content to sit in the corner with a coke and a plate of nachos and watch my severely extroverted wife joyfully flit around the room like a hummingbird talking to everyone. That extroverted personality is simply not my way.

For example, while we were living in Arizona, I made a decision one Sunday morning that I was going to be extroverted and outwardly happy and joyful at church. So in between class and the worship service, I was walking through the halls glad-handing people and slapping people on the back and "Hey, how ya doin?" everyone. When I got to April who was already sitting in the church pew with two of our very young sons, I was literally sweating and on the edge of hyperventilating.

She said, "What's wrong?"

I took a quick drink from one of the kids' juice boxes and in between deep breaths, I said, "I was trying to be nice to people."

With God as my witness, she said, "Honey, you know you have to be careful when you do that."

To me, crowds of more than three or four people are claustrophobic. At parties and such, I will usually talk to a few people; but I have a hard time being in a crowd and filling two hours with superficial conversation, especially if the person I'm talking to doesn't like sports or meat cooked on a grill. But, whether you are an introvert or extrovert, nobody wants to be alone all the time. It's not healthy. Human beings are wired for relationships. We are wired for community and connectedness. And yet, so often we find ourselves...alone.

I am reminded of a lesson a teacher taught in a church class when I was very young. She had plucked a large leaf off a sycamore tree just before church. When she showed it to us in class a short time later, it still looked green and fresh. The next Sunday, the leaf had begun to dry out just a bit. With each passing week that the leaf was away from its natural source of nourishment on the tree, the leaf became drier and more discolored. It eventually turned brown and dry and began to fall apart. The teacher made the analogy that this is what people are like when they are away from people who love and care for them, away from the church, and away from the supportive benefits of community and relationships.

That is a simple illustration, but isn't it amazing that the simple ones are the ones we remember the most? There are times we feel like that leaf—away from our source of strength and alone.

There are times when we are alone when there is simply nobody else around. Then, there are times when we are alone in a crowd, surrounded by people we don't know, surrounded by people we have nothing in common with, or, do I dare say, surrounded by people we don't care about or, we are pretty sure, who don't care about us.

Alone. It's one of those words that, depending on your stage in life and circumstances, can be seen as a blessing or a curse. To the person who needs contact with many people, the idea of being alone is painful. But there are other times where being alone is of great benefit.

Alone.

This was probably twenty-five to thirty years ago, but I was having a conversation with a preacher who was about to take a one-month sabbatical. I was jokingly asking him what he was going to do with all of that free time. I figured he would talk about golfing, fishing, or traveling the world. He said, "I'm going to spend some time with my family; but mainly I'm going to go camping. I just need to go and be alone with God for a while." I remember thinking, *Why would a preacher, who spends every week preparing sermons and Bible classes, need to be alone with God? Isn't that what you do all week, every week?* Remember this was twenty-five to thirty years ago. I was young and naïve, and life hadn't yet given me the experience to understand the need for physical and spiritual rest.

Ever since that day, I have often thought about being alone with God. Why would someone intentionally want to be alone with God? What does it even mean to be alone with God?

While working on my master's in Bible and family ministry, I took a class titled "Preaching from the Book of Genesis." Genesis is really a book about getting acquainted with God, and there is a particular story I want to consider. In Genesis 31, we see the familiar story of Jacob and his large family leaving Laban. After many years of isolation, they were heading back to the land of Jacob's fathers and relatives. They were going home—home to community, home to relationships. Jacob could see his mother and father that he hadn't seen in so many years. He could introduce them to their daughters-in-law and grandchildren. And I must wonder, as Joseph was his most beloved, *Would Jacob introduce Joseph first or "save the best for last"?*

All the years. All the stories. Time. Home. Excitement.

However, the reality of home also means seeing his brother Esau. Twenty-plus years of running from deceit was coming to a head, and it likely meant Jacob's death.

We all know of the incident many years earlier when Jacob and his mother, Rebekah, tricked Isaac and secured the blessing intended for the elder Esau.[29] We read that Jacob had to flee his homeland because Esau said he would kill him as soon as Isaac died.[30] Two decades had passed, but Jacob understood the long lifespan of anger and resentment and was convinced Esau wanted him dead. It makes you wonder why Jacob would take this risk at all. I guess the call of "home" was too strong. In chapter 32, Jacob and his family had traveled for a distance and made their way to the banks of the Jabbok River. Soon, Jacob would have to confront Esau and his four hundred men. Jacob had separated his family into two protective groups and had had his servants deliver gifts to Esau. "Gifts" is a gentle word for "bribes." Night began to fall, and Jacob thought of the coming events of tomorrow.

Now, put yourself in Jacob's shoes. If you thought you were likely to be killed tomorrow morning, what would you do?

---

[29] Genesis 27
[30] Genesis 27:41 (ESV)

- Wouldn't you want to spend time with your family and friends?

- Wouldn't you want to tell them how much you love them and share fond memories?

- What would be your last meal? Animal-style In-N-Out burgers? Or would you grill up a two-inch-thick Hawaiian rib eye with a loaded baked potato?

- Maybe you would spend time with your family to impart any last words of wisdom.

- Maybe you would talk to your spouse about life insurance policies, bank accounts, or whatever else it takes to "get your house in order."

It seems like you would do anything and everything to keep from being alone...wouldn't you? But that's not what Jacob did. He left his family and walked back across the river...to be alone.

Was it a cool, foggy, eerie night full of suspense? Or was the night air clean and clear with full visibility of God's grandeur in the moon and stars? The events that happened that night were miraculous and changed not only the life of Jacob but the entire nation of Israel. There are many Bible scholars who declare this night in the life of Jacob as the seminal point in all of the Bible and the nation of Israel. Think about how much the history of the ongoing world is put in motion on this night.

Jacob was alone, or so he thought. A mysterious man showed up out of nowhere and began to fight with Jacob.[31] Why? To be honest, since we know the end of the story, it is kind of humorous. Jacob was sitting alone on a log just pondering life. All of a sudden, a man showed up and wanted to fight. What on earth must Jacob have been thinking when this happened?

We learn later this man was an angel, or a representation of God. It is such a strange story, but it is a great story. And what is so amazing is that Jacob had no idea any of this was going to happen as

---

[31] Genesis 32:22–30

he settled in for a night of solitude. All he knew was that his sandals were wet from crossing the river and he was alone.

I wonder what he was doing as he was alone.

- Was he reflecting on his life, thinking back on a life overflowing with joys and sorrows?
- Was he thinking about Esau and how he had so deeply hurt him? Esau had made a foolish trade for a bowl of stew,[32] but why would Jacob ultimately hurt his brother like that? For what? Material things?
- Was he thinking about how he hurt his father, Isaac? Why would he intentionally hurt his father so deeply?
- Was he thinking about his relationship with his mother, Rebekah, and did he understand what they had done together to trick Isaac was wrong? Did he make up his mind that he would talk to her about that day so long ago and confront the deceit that had altered so many lives?
- Was he praying?
- Was he bargaining with God?
- Was he asking God for guidance or forgiveness?
- Was he wondering if God loved him or even cared about him?
- Why did Jacob want to be alone with God?
- Why did my preacher friend want to be alone with God?

I look through the Bible for answers, for wisdom. I begin to look at the main characters of the Bible, people who have an impact on the history of Christianity and the world—our heroes and sometimes even our villains. Look at their times of impact, and look at how those times seem to be in proximity to a time of being alone with God. It might be a short time of aloneness with God, such as when God asked Cain, "Where is Abel your brother?"[33] Or it could

---

[32] Genesis 25:34
[33] Genesis 4:9

be an extended time such as the three years Paul spent in Arabia after his conversion.[34]

- God was alone with Adam in the Garden of Eden; and it was good.[35]
- God gave blueprints of a rather large boat to a completely confused Noah.[36]
- After an elderly Abraham had to check the battery in his hearing aid, God told him that he would have a child and would be the patriarch of a great nation. God was met with laughter and disbelief.[37]
- God called Moses to a burning bush in an isolated countryside and told him that he was going to be a great leader[38] and then later on Mt. Sinai when God gave Moses the Ten Commandments.[39]
- God passed by Elijah as he dwelt in a cave.[40]
- God spent years with the disciple his Son loved on an island called Patmos and helped him write a book simply known as "Revelation."

Alone.

Think of the times where someone cried out to the Lord in loneliness and despair.

- Hagar went out alone and pleaded with God for the safety of her son Ishmael.[41]

---

[34] Galatians 1:17
[35] Genesis 2:25
[36] Genesis 6:9–22
[37] Genesis 17:15–17
[38] Exodus 3
[39] Exodus 19:1 to 20:17
[40] 1 Kings 11:19
[41] Genesis 21:16–21

- A once proud but now broken and blind Sampson sat in chains and begged God for just one more day of strength.[42]
- In a parable spoken by Jesus, the hungry prodigal son pleaded with God as he shamefully wrestled a dirty half-eaten corncob away from the hungry pigs.[43]

Alone.

Think of someone who is alone with God in the midst of a crowd.

- Jacob's young son, Joseph, sat captive in a caravan wondering why his brothers had betrayed him and sold him to strangers.[44]
- And several years later, a falsely accused Joseph again sat in a jail cell and called on God for insight to dreams.[45]
- Daniel knelt in front of a window for all to see and defied the rulers of the land while boldly praying to God.[46]
- Stephen stood before the high priests with a face like that of an angel, just before he was struck with the first stone.[47]
- Paul on the road to Damascus was on his hands and knees feeling the hardpacked dirt of the road under his blind eyes.[48]

Alone.

Think of the times when someone was alone with God and the conversation was not so pleasant.

---

[42] Judges 16:28
[43] Luke 15:16
[44] Genesis 37:28
[45] Genesis 40:23
[46] Daniel 6:10–18
[47] Acts 7
[48] Acts 9:8

- Jonah defied God and God said, "So you don't want to do what I've asked you to do. Let's spend a few days together in the belly of a fish and think about it."[49]
- Job finally became frustrated and angry with God, and an irritated God said, "So you think you know so much, and you want to complain about your lot in life. Let's spend some time together so that I can ask you a few questions."[50]

Alone.

I think of my preacher friend with his tent pitched under some tall pine trees on the edge of a cold creek. He sits on a worn-out log at a small campfire, alone with God. He was intentional. He wanted to be alone with God.

- Was he frustrated with God like Job and wanted to complain?
- Was he telling God that his task of leading the church and all of his responsibilities was too big like Moses?
- Was he telling God he felt all alone even in the midst of the large congregation he served?
- Was he telling God he was tired and worn out and needed some strength?
- Was he pleading for the lives and well-being of his family?
- Was he praying for relationships?
- Was he angry at God for something?
- Was he praying for wisdom and enlightenment?
- Was he thanking God for his unending love and mercy?
- Was he asking God for strength and wisdom to lead the church and to be a faithful conduit of the Holy Word?
- Was this a time of confession?
- Was this a time of humility and selflessness?
- Was this a time of weakness and vulnerability?

---

[49] Jonah 1:17
[50] Job 38–41

- Was this a time of full-hearted praise and worship?
- Was it a time of longing for a relationship with the Creator?
- Was he reading the Psalms where David wrote, "Be still and know that I am God"[51]?

Was it all of these or none of these? Had my preacher friend stepped in the creek, and were his shoes wet like Jacob's?

Alone.

I think of being alone with God on a dark, foggy hillside. I see Christ as he thinks of the coming events of tomorrow. He pleads with God, "Is there another way?" He is so tired and weary. He is humble. He is scared. He is sad. He is sovereign. He is all powerful. Yet, he says, "Your will be done."[52] His submission to his Father leads to the cruel cross where he cries out, *"Eloi, Eloi, lema sabachthani?"*[53]

Alone.

Jacob had spent the night wrestling with God, and his hip was injured. Early the next morning, he was limping[54] badly as he crossed the Jabbok River. He broke through the brush at the river's edge, and his eyes met the unmistakable figure of his brother Esau. Jacob was humble, helpless, penitent, and blessed. He was changed. He was forgiven. He was joyful. He was the leader of a great nation. The crowds in attendance simply saw a lonely man limping. They had no idea he was walking with God.

I am struck by another time God was walking with someone. In Genesis, God was alone with Adam, and God must have loved this relationship of undivided oneness. But he knew Adam needed to be with someone compatible, and God's love for Adam required him to do something that would diminish this relationship. Genesis 2:18

---

[51] Psalm 46:10
[52] Matthew 26:39
[53] Matthew 27:46
[54] Genesis 32:31

says, "Then the LORD God said, 'It is not good that the man should be alone; I will make him a helper fit for him.'" So God created Eve, and immediately God's relationship with his creation was altered. Instead of being alone with Adam, there was now another person who would divert much of Adam's attention. But God still enjoyed his time with both Adam and Eve as they walked together in the Garden of Eden. We then read that Satan deceived Eve and caused sin to enter the world, and the God–man relationship was forever altered. Genesis 3 tells of God walking through the garden, but he could not find Adam and Eve because they were hiding as they realized they were naked. We then encounter the first recorded question ever asked by God, "Where are you?"[55]

I have been trying to think of instances where Satan has been overcome with joy. One obviously was the torture and crucifixion of Jesus, when Satan thought he had defeated the Son of God. I believe another time of joy for Satan was hearing God ask this question, "Where are you?" With sin, Satan was amused at the corruption of God's creation.

I wonder, *Does Satan draw that same joy when we, in our times of despair, call out to God, "Where are you?"* The times we feel like God has abandoned us or the times I felt he had more important things to do than help me in my painful struggles. We search our minds and wonder, *Have I done something to make God angry with me? Is that why I'm enduring so much pain and hurt?* Has my sin and darkness been so great that God's disappointment reached a point where he doesn't care and is leaving me…alone?

I also wonder about another time where Satan must have experienced joy. It was night on the Sea of Galilee where the disciples were on a boat fighting a brutal storm. The day had been long, and they were exhausted as they rowed the oars hard trying to keep course. Fear and excitement entered the boat as they thought they saw Jesus walking on the water. "Could that really be Jesus, or is it a ghost?" "How can this be, out here in this storm?" Shocked and amazed, they

---

[55] Genesis 3:9 (ESV)

must have stopped rowing as they were trying to figure out what was happening.

Peter saw Jesus walking on the water, and he wanted to join him. And, instead of getting out of the boat himself, he asked Jesus to ask him to come out. When Jesus asked him to come out into the storm with him, Peter climbed over the rail of the boat and reached his foot for the water. Can you imagine the full range of emotion Peter felt when his foot found a firm foundation...on water?

Miraculously, Peter began to walk toward Jesus. He had left the relative security of the boat and was now willingly walking through the waves of an angry sea. As he walked toward Jesus, he began to get distracted. He thought of the wind and waves. He thought of the impossibility of what was happening. He thought he would be safe if he turned back to the boat, but as he turned around, he saw the boat drifting away as it was being pushed by the storm and the other disciples were no longer rowing as they chose to watch instead. He turned back and looked at the sea. The storm was brought on by cold air rushing down onto the warm water; and now that cold air was hitting Peter, and he began to shiver, and his fingertips became painful. The gusts of wind blew the water into his face and eyes, so he held his hands up to block the irritating water. He was wet and cold. His friends were drifting away in the boat. He was discouraged and scared. He was uncomfortable. Thoughts of Jesus the Savior standing in front of him had left his mind as he was now concentrating on the effects of the storm. As the waves crashed into his soaked legs and body, he began to feel vulnerable. Convinced that this was impossible, he began to sink into the sea.

Have you ever considered that that moment is exactly where Satan wants you to live? The moment when you feel uncomfortable, vulnerable, and all alone. The moment when your eyes are on everything except Jesus. In the midst of a miracle, Satan wants our minds to live in fear, doubt, and loneliness.

Satan loves it when you are struggling, and you begin to doubt your abilities and talents. He loves it when you begin to wonder if your spouse and children are embarrassed by your shortcomings. He loves it when you wonder if your family still loves you and is proud of you or if your parents and siblings are shaking their heads in disdain for the situation "you brought on yourself." He loves it when your mind convinces you that your friends have abandoned you, even though they really haven't. He loves it when you're uncomfortable and irritated and discouraged. He loves it when you let your discouragement lead to unhealthy habits. He loves it when you look in the mirror and see a failure. He loves it when your attention is on anything and everything except Jesus. He loves it when you wonder if Jesus still loves you and why he refuses to help as you stand in the storm that he himself called you into.

The setting of this storm is the Sea of Galilee. It was only a short time ago, in this very same body of water, that Peter experienced his greatest professional and financial triumph. This was the sea where Peter obeyed the miraculous words of Jesus and set his nets in the water again and pulled in the largest catch of fish he had ever caught.[56] It was a time of pure joy and exhilaration and wonder. He was in fact in the middle of another miraculous event on that same water, but now he was sinking. Fear and doubt crept in like a dark-hearted assassin.

Do you ever wonder about the genesis of words and phrases and verses? I like to think that the disciples and apostles would often get together and share stories about their journeys and their ministries. Can you even begin to imagine all they experienced? I can see them rolling with laughter at some stories while crying in anguish and sorrow over others. I can see them speaking with awe about things they had seen and done, and I would imagine there were many times when people would ask about their time with Jesus. I can see Paul sitting in a group of the apostles and asking rapid-fire question after question about things Jesus had said and done. What a mixture of emotions would be generated with these stories. Can you imagine the number of questions Paul had and then follow-up questions when he heard something that piqued his interest?

I see the men and women sitting around a table and Andrew tapping Peter on the shoulder and saying, "Hey, tell Paul about the time you walked on water."

---

[56] Luke 4:33–41

"You did what? You walked on water?" Paul replies in wonder and a tinge of doubt.

Peter, almost sheepishly, answers, "Yeah, for a little while."

Paul senses some hesitancy on Peter's part and quietly asks, "For a little while? What does that mean?"

Andrew starts laughing and waving his arms around like someone losing their balance. "Yeah, then he started to sink." All the other apostles laugh a somewhat uneasy laugh because they know it was a time of joy, but it was also painful for Peter in the moment.

To save Peter's pride, Matthew says, "I didn't see you out there walking on the water, Andrew."

"I could have if I wanted to," Andrew replies.

"I doubt that," quips Thomas.

Paul isn't sure what's happening with this back and forth between the apostles, but he does want to know what happened as he asks Peter, "You started to sink? Why? How did you—"

He doesn't finish his question when Peter quietly interrupts, "I started to look at the storm. I got scared. Discouraged." With his head bowed slightly, Peter motions toward the other apostles, "I wanted to get back to the boat, but when I looked back at them, they were floating away. I just felt all alone out there. I...I took my eyes off Jesus."

Peter and the other apostles then tell Paul the entire story in great detail. They talk of the storm being one of the worst they had ever seen. One of them openly wonders if Jesus had sent them out there to set them up for this event. They talk of fear and weariness. They talk of their admiration for Peter and his willingness to climb over the edge even as they were telling him not to as it was sure suicide. Paul sits in awe-inspired wonder as he listens to the power of our mighty Lord. Paul hugs Peter and tearfully says, "Wish I could have seen that, brother."

How many times in his life did Paul think of that story? How many times did he tell that story and emphasize the need to keep your eyes on Jesus?

Some people believe Paul wrote the Book of Hebrews. Others believe it was a protégé of Paul's such as Pricilla or Aquila. Whether it was Paul or one of the others, do you think this story was on their mind when they wrote in Hebrews 12:2–3, "Let us fix our eyes on Jesus, the author and perfecter of our faith, who for the joy set before him endured the cross, scorning its shame, and sat down at the right hand of the throne of God. Consider him who endured such opposition from sinful men, so that you will not grow weary and lose heart."

Satan is a liar, and he finds immense joy when he clouds our minds and makes us feel as if God has abandoned us and left us alone. Satan knows the truth and he tries to hide it, and he tries to hide the significance of a name.

The truth is revealed in the birth story of Jesus. Matthew chapter 1 describes the mental struggles Joseph experienced as he tried to come to grips with the pregnancy of his virgin fiancé, Mary:

> And her husband Joseph, being a just man and unwilling to put her to shame, resolved to divorce her quietly. But as he considered these things, behold an angel of the Lord appeared to him in a dream, saying, "Joseph, son of David, do not fear to take Mary as your wife, for that which is conceived in her is from the Holy Spirit. She will bear a son, and you shall call his name Jesus, for he will save his people from their sins." All this took place to fulfill what the Lord had spoken by the prophet:
> "Behold, the virgin shall conceive and bear a son, and they shall call his name Immanuel" (which means, God with us).[57]

This was the fulfillment of the prophecy made in Isaiah 7:14.

Of all of the names of Jesus, this is the one I like the most—Immanuel, "God with us." I am never alone.

Alone. What a strange word. Depending on circumstances and mind-set, it can signify either sadness or joy. But, to the Christian, is alone even possible? I think of the disciples when their time with Jesus

---

[57] Matthew 1:20–23 (ESV)

was coming to an end. Jesus chose twelve ordinary men to take on a herculean task: change the world forever. But Jesus knew they were going to experience intense trials and tribulations. They would face pain and persecution. They would experience frustration and discouragement as they often felt their task was too great. Some of these men had families, and their wives[58] and children were going to be pulled into the turmoil and distress. Have you ever tried to put yourself in their shoes and thought about the magnitude of their charge? Isn't it interesting how Jesus concluded his time with them? When he was giving them the Great Commission, he ended by saying, "And behold, I am with you always, to the end of the age."[59] Then in Acts 1, the very last thing Jesus ever said to the apostles was that the Holy Spirit would be their companion.[60] Do you see what Jesus was saying? The last thing he ever said to his friends here on earth was "You will never be alone."

Every day of the school year, I drove by the elementary school and looked under the big tree. I looked for the young boy standing by himself dressed different from the other kids. Except for that first day, I never saw him again. Or maybe I saw him many times but never recognized him. I would often think to myself, *I hope he has friends. I hope he is joyful. I hope he got to play in the game. I hope his clothes got dirty and his hair got messed up.*

But, above all else, I hope someday he taps into the strength, glory, wisdom, and joy of the God who is calling out for him. I hope he truly realizes that he is never alone.

My prayer is the same for you. You are not alone.

Immanuel

---

[58] Matthew 8:14
[59] Matthew 28:20
[60] Acts 1:8

I am the vine; you are the branches. If a man
remains in me, and I in him, he will bear much
fruit; apart from me you can do nothing.
(John 15:5)

Chapter 5

The Door

You can laugh, or you can cry.

When financial times are hard, it seems like car trouble can treat you like a baby treats a diaper. Our main family car was a burgundy-colored Toyota Previa van. It had been a wonderful car that had carried us around the country for over three hundred thousand miles. But it was beginning to break down.

We first noticed the decline when driving down Central Expressway in Dallas. The traffic was flowing, and we were going sixty-five or seventy miles an hour, and all a sudden the car started slowing down. My foot was still on the gas pedal, but we were slowing down. I began to frantically look over the dash at all the gauges. No lights were flashing, and nothing was buzzing. The engine was still running, but we were decelerating. April asked why I was slowing down, and I had no answer. I made my way over to the right-hand lane and was trying to figure out how to safely pull off to the side of the road and get to an off-ramp. The speedometer made its way down to 18 mph. The off-ramp was in sight about a mile ahead. When we got within a few hundred yards, the van inexplicably started gaining speed. It made its way back up to sixty-five and ran like nothing at all was wrong. Since we had no money for repairs, we simply kept driving the car and waited for the occasional drop in speed. It would sometimes go for weeks between occurrences, but we always had to be prepared and stayed close to the right lane.

Then, "the slow start" became a problem. The slow start occurred when leaving a stop sign or red light, and the van would get to 4 mph and stay there. No matter how hard you pressed the gas, it would glide along at 4 mph for a few hundred feet and then speed up. This is usually when you find out if the people behind you have a functioning car horn as they think it is necessary to let you know that "4" might not be the optimal speed for this particular stretch of road. They would honk and, whenever possible, angrily pass you while indicating whether or not they had had a manicure on their middle finger. The slow start was never predictable, and the kids would cheer when there was a clean getaway.

We never had any idea when the van would slow down on the highway or slow start, but it was always an adventure. The kids were especially traumatized by the slow start because it would often happen at the school parking lot. The kids would hide down low in the seats trying to seek anonymity, but everyone knew whom the van belonged to.

As I said, the van had over three hundred thousand miles on it, and the sliding door had been opened and shut countless times, and the track on the top of the door began to wear out. Consequently, the door would sometimes catch or act like it was going to come unseated. It finally got to the point where we had to open it very carefully and only to about eighteen-inches wide. The kids would then slide out sideways through the opening. This again was a source of trauma and embarrassment when they exited the car at school.

It was May, which is graduation season. Our oldest nephew was graduating from high school in Mansfield, Texas, and his parents (my oldest brother and his wife) were throwing a graduation party at their country club. They had rented out the entire facility on a Saturday night and had invited many family and friends. Our kids were excited to see all the family and get to go swimming at the country club pool with the slide and big diving board. Apparently, the diving board on our pool wasn't springy enough for them.

We were asked to show up a little early to help set up for the party, which we were glad to do. We drove over an hour and a half through Dallas traffic from Celina to Mansfield; not once did the car drop to 18 mph. We pulled into the parking lot which luckily only had a few cars in it at this point. Several parking spots away, my middle brother, Kenneth, and his family had just pulled in as well. Their son, Aaron, excitedly came running over to our van, grabbed the door handle, and slid it open. He did not hear the yells of "Nooooo!" warning him of the danger. The door slid open, made a loud pop, and fell off the van and onto the asphalt of the empty parking space next to the car. Aaron looked mortified, as did our kids. Everyone froze and stared at the door lying next to the car. April and I got out of the van and walked to where the door lay on the ground. Aaron was apologizing profusely, and our kids were still in the car not knowing what to do. April and I stood there for a few seconds and began to start laughing uncontrollably. Between the looks on Aaron and the kids' faces, the sight of a door lying on the ground, and the gaping hole in the side of the van where the door was supposed to be, it was truly a hilarious scene.

In moments like these, you have two choices. You can laugh or cry. We chose to laugh.

While the kids could not figure out why we were laughing, their main concern was getting inside the building and away from this embarrassing scene. I told them to go inside and help set up for the party, and they took off running like they were being chased by a lion.

April and I stood there looking at the door, laughing and wondering what else could go wrong. Then it started. You would be amazed at how many people can walk up on a scene where a door is lying on the ground next to a car and ask, "Did your door come off?" The first was Kenneth. It was his son who brought the door to the pavement.

"Did your door come off?"

"Kind of looks that way, doesn't it?" I replied.

He asks, "You going to put it back on?"

It was a question that not only amazed me but created concern as well. Yes, of course, I was going to put it back on. Do you think I was going to drive eighteen miles an hour all the way back to Celina with no door? But I honestly had no idea how I was going to accomplish the task. Not only did I have no tools but I also had no automotive knowledge whatsoever. I'm the sucker every mechanic loves to have in their shop. They could tell me the reason the car was going 18 mph was because "the smooter valve is stuck in the nipple slip," and I would pay several hundred dollars to fix it. Now, I had to put a sliding door back on a van, with no tools and no knowledge and in a parking lot of a country club that was about to be teaming with traffic.

I looked in the back of the van and found the following: a twenty-six-inch aluminum Mark McGwire big barrel t-ball bat, one black size 8 left woman's shoe commonly called a "pump," an old dried-out half bag of French fries from a McDonald's happy meal, and a hanger used for slacks with the cardboard tube—and of course, the tube was bent. That's it. That's what I had to work with.

I started by trying to prop the door up into place. It was heavy and awkward. I got it in place to slide into the track, and it fell off. I got it back in place, and it fell off. I was beginning to see this as a potential pattern.

"Hey, did your door fall off?" I heard in the distance.

I had now spent close to an hour trying to get the door back on the track. The parking lot was getting full, except for the space next to my car which I had protected from countless people trying to pull into the prime spot on the front row.

My nerves were frayed. I was tired, sweaty, and embarrassed. I could hear the party taking place on the other side of the brick walls. I heard the music, the laughter, and the kids joyfully splashing in the pool. And I heard the familiar sound of the van door falling to the asphalt again.

The timing was terrible. I was ready to snap, and she was entitled. I was trying to get the door back in place when I was startled by a short quick car honk. I turned my head to see an elderly woman in a brand-new Lexus angling into the parking spot, and she was signaling for me to get out of the way. I leaned the door against the side of the van and walked over and tried to explain to her that I was trying to get the door back on and it would not be safe for her to park there in case the door fell off. She looked at me and then to the van and then back to me. With an air of superiority, she slightly tossed her head back and let out a little snort of derision. The only thing lacking was her saying, "You peasant!" This snort sent me over the top. Here I was trying to keep her car from getting damaged and she snorted me. So, being the adult, I did the mature thing and crossed my arms and snorted her back. The only problem was when I snorted, I felt something dislodge from my left nostril and almost immediately felt something hit my left forearm. I looked down, and sitting on my arm was a booger somewhere between the size of a dime and a small Frisbee. I quickly tried to knock the green behemoth away, but she had seen it. A slight Cruella de Vil smile of evil satisfaction crept onto her thin lips as she put the car in reverse and pulled away. A controlled rage set in, but I must admit that if I would have had the twenty-six-inch aluminum Mark McGwire big barrel t-ball bat in my hand at the time, I would likely be writing this from a prison cell.

Apparently, she went to the party and tattled on me, because a few minutes later, Lewis came out. He was the one who was throwing the party for his son.

He said, "Why'd you take the door off your car?"

I looked at him and said, "Well, you know, Lewis, I figured today was as good a time as any to do a little general automotive repair, so I took the door off."

He apparently didn't catch my truckload of sarcasm as he replied, "Well, put it back on and get into the party."

After another fifteen or twenty minutes, I finally got an idea of how to leverage the door against the frame and shimmy the wheels back in the track. Using the twenty-six-inch aluminum Mark McGwire big barrel t-ball bat, I bent the frame enough to let the wheel bracket slide in. I swear there was a distinct sound of angels singing when the door slid back on the frame and closed. However, I was afraid the door would slide back off due to the area where I bent the frame. So I took the twenty-six-inch aluminum Mark McGwire big barrel t-ball bat and started hitting the door frame to bend the metal back into place. With my left hand, I held the door in place. With my right hand crossing over my left, I was pounding the side of the van with the twenty-six-inch aluminum Mark McGwire big barrel t-ball bat. *Boom! Boom! Boom!* It's working. A distant harp started playing, and the angels were now singing in unison with the banging of the twenty-six-inch aluminum Mark McGwire big barrel t-ball bat. The frame was bending back in place and should hold the door.

Out of the corner of my left eye, I saw another car trying to pull into the spot. I turned and looked at the man and woman in the front seat. They had kids in the back seat, and I assumed they were here for the party. I locked eyes with the lovely mom in the passenger seat. A look of fear came over her face, and she started pounding her right hand on the dash and yelling, "*Go! Go! Go!*" Her husband quickly pulled away from the prized parking spot being guarded by the sweaty mad man, wielding a twenty-six-inch aluminum Mark McGwire t-ball bat.

It took a few minutes to bend the frame enough to where I felt comfortable that it would hold the door. I thought, *A few more smacks and it'll be done. Boom. Boom.* "Freeze, fat man!" The yell startled me. *Freeze, fat man? What does that mean?* I turned and saw the country club security cop sitting in his golf cart, and he was shining a twelve-inch black metal flashlight at my face even though the sun was still out. Turns out, the lady in the previous car had told the security officer there was someone in the parking lot bashing cars with a twenty-six-inch aluminum Mark McGwire big barrel t-ball bat. He came to check it out.

Now I'll admit I could stand to lose a few pounds. But this guy had two cans of Pringles and a Burger King bag in the seat next to him and a sixty-four-ounce Big Gulp cup wedged in the cupholder. He was easily tipping three hundo pounds, and he was yelling, "Freeze, fat man!" I recognized he was bigger than me, but I quickly realized I had the advantage in fancy footwork, and my metal weapon of choice was fourteen inches longer than his. That, along with the adrenaline-packed rage I'd had for the last hour, gave me a great advantage in this upcoming fight. Just before metal was about to fly, Lewis came walking out to the car and exasperatingly asked what was going on. Apparently, he had overheard someone talking about a "lunatic smashing cars in the parking lot." He explained to fat Barney Fife who I was and what was happening with the door. The security guard left, and Lewis told me again to get into the party.

I put the twenty-six-inch aluminum Mark McGwire big barrel t-ball bat in the back of the van next to the woman's size 8 pump. I walked into the party and started looking for April to tell her the tale of my automotive triumph, but I doubted she would believe me. I finally spotted her, but quickly assessed a problem. She was talking to the old lady in the Lexus who snorted me. I coolly made my way down the hall and into the men's restroom. One glance in the mirror and I began to understand why the lady thought I was crazy. I was covered in sweat. My hair was disheveled. My white polo golf shirt and tan shorts were both smeared with sweat, dirt, and grease. I won't go into the whole story, but looking back on it now, I realize I should have cleaned my shirt and then cleaned my pants rather than taking them off and cleaning them both at the same time in a restroom frequently visited by partygoers.

The rest of the party was uneventful. It was a good time. When the party was over, we stayed to help clean up. It was almost midnight when we headed to the van to drive home. I explained to April and the kids what I had done to the door and told them they could not open that door ever again. They climbed in through the front passenger door and got their seats.

A soft voice came from behind me, "What if the door falls off while we're driving home? Will it suck us out?" The kids had seen too many airplane disaster movies, but it was a valid question. I looked at April, and she just raised her eyebrows and smiled a nervous and questioning smile.

"No. It will be all right." I answered confidently to reassure them everything was okay. I then added, "But, Garrett, why don't you hold the door handle just to make sure it doesn't pop out?"

He looked at me like I was crazy and said, "Well, what if it pulls me out with it?" Another valid question. He apparently was fixated on being sucked out of the moving car.

"Oh, it will be okay. We might not even get above 18 mph on the way home." I thought the joke would lighten the mood and get his attention on something else. By the look on his face, I could tell Garrett wasn't reassured, amused, or distracted.

"Jacob, you sit next to Garrett and wrap your arms around him so he doesn't get sucked out."

Jacob asked, "Well, what if it sucks us both out?"

Wondering why there was such an obsession with being sucked out of the car, I wanted to tell him to quit being selfish, but instead said, "There's no way it will suck you both out." I'm not sure why I said that so confidently. I guess I figured the laws of probability would make it a long shot that they would both get sucked out if they were both wearing seatbelts. Surprisingly, it apparently worked as Jacob began wrapping his arms around Garrett's waist.

As all that discussion was taking place, Brooks began to cheer from the back seat. "What are you cheering about?" I asked.

"We got past 4 mph without going slow," he said happily.

"Hey, what do you know?" I hadn't been paying attention as we were pulling away, but sure enough, we had gone through the empty parking lot without the slow start. Things were looking up.

We got on the highway, and April said, "You should probably drive in the right lane in case the door falls off. We don't want it landing in the middle of the road and causing a wreck."

"Smart thinking," I said with a nod of approval. I wanted to add, *Yeah. That way the boys also won't get run over if they get sucked out.* However, before I said that, I turned and saw the panicked look on Garrett's face and the Vulcan death grip he had on the door handle. So I decided that could be left unsaid.

We made it home safe, no problems at all with unexpected speed reductions or doors falling off.

The next day, two interesting things happened. First, I went to Home Depot and bought some welding glue and several rolls of duct tape. I welded the door shut and wrapped duct tape on the inside of the door just to be double sure it wouldn't pop off again. It took a long time to do the tape on the inside. I could have easily done it on the outside, but that would look tacky, especially by the part of the door frame that was smashed up by the twenty-six-inch aluminum Mark McGwire big barrel t-ball bat.

The second thing that happened that day took place at the baseball field for some batting practice and fungo. Garrett had a terrible day. His swing was off, and he had a lot of trouble throwing the ball from shortstop to first. He said his arm was sore, which I initially attributed to several hours of swimming the night before. However, after thinking it through a bit more, I realized his right arm was probably fatigued from the hour-and-a-half death grip he had on the door handle the night before while trying to keep from getting sucked out onto the pavement of the LBJ Freeway.

We continued to use the van as our family car. The kids would enter and exit through the front doors or through the back door. One day, I walked in on a conversation April was having with one of the kids. I heard the loud exclamation, "It's not funny, Mom!" as the child stomped angrily away.

"What's that about?" I asked.

"Oh, the kids are upset because everyone calls us 'the clown car.'"

"What?"

"The kids at school call our van the clown car because when we pull up, the kids pile out of the car like it's the clown car at the circus."

We both had a great laugh at that image.

It got worse though. Over time, the back door began to wear out from the constant raising and lowering. The hinge and lock began to come loose, so we had to run a bungee cord from the bumper to the handle to keep the door shut. I came home one day to the sound of a slamming bedroom door and April laughing.

"What's so funny?" I asked.

"Well, we're not 'the clown car' anymore. We are now 'the thong car.'"

"What does that mean?"

"The kids at school say our van looks like it's wearing thong underwear with the bungee cord, so we're the thong car now."

Again, we had a good laugh at that, even as the embarrassment was apparently scarring our kids' lives forever.

*****

Milton Berle once said, "Laughter is an instant vacation."[61] Isn't that true? Laughter has a way of taking you to a place of joy even when happiness seems to be the furthest thing from your mind.

I've been thinking about going through times of deep trial, and you basically have two choices: You can laugh or cry. There were many times April and I were at the end of our rope and would tearfully ask in exasperation, "Can anything else happen to us?" But there were also times when something bad would happen and we would simply laugh. Often people would ask why we were laughing over something clearly not enjoyable. The answer was simple: "Because right now, it's better than crying." Little did I know the truth to that statement.

I am more and more aware of God's amazing creation when I think about how he made us and the simple fact that God made us to laugh and cry. There are times when a good cleansing cry is what we need. The October 7, 2017, issue of *Medical News Today* contains an article titled "Eight benefits of crying: Why it's good to shed a few tears." Three of the eight reasons deal with chemical responses in the body that occur when crying:

1. Crying activates the parasympathetic nervous system which causes a self-soothing effect on people.
2. Tears release oxytocin and endorphins which ease physical and emotional pain and promote a sense of well-being.
3. Tears contain a number of stress hormones and other chemicals that researchers believe reduces stress.

Research also discovered the many benefits of laughing. A quick internet search provides myriad articles about the numerous physical, mental, emotional, and spiritual benefits of laughter. One article by the University of Rochester Medical Center, titled "Laughter is Good Medicine,"[62] was interesting. While this is not a hardcore medical

---

[61] "Laughter is Good Medicine." University of Rochester Medical Center. Wichtowski, Lorraine. April 19, 2018. Urmc.rochester.edu

[62] "Laughter is Good Medicine." University of Rochester Medical Center. Wichtowski, Lorraine. April 19, 2018. Urmc.rochester.edu

descriptor, it does lay out several important thoughts. For example, "When you laugh out loud, you can't be anxious, sad, angry, or even just blah. Laughter is pure joy; but it is more than that. Laughter is good medicine." Several remarkable points about the benefits of laughter include the following:

1. Studies show that laughter and a good sense of humor can literally ward off or at least diminish disease.
2. Dr. Sven Svebak of the Norwegian University of Science and Technology tracked 54,000 Norwegians for seven years and discovered that those individuals who found life the funniest lived longer.
3. In 2015, the journal *Psychosomatic Medicine* published the "15-Year Follow-Up Study of Sense of Humor and Causes of Mortality." The study of 53,000 people found a sense of humor was positively associated with survival for people with cardiovascular disease and infections.
4. Other studies have shown that hearty laughter, just like exercise, decreases arterial stiffness, contributes to better blood sugar regulation in diabetics, and can improve cancer-killing cells.
5. The real benefit of humor, however, is cumulative. Finding humor in everyday life over the course of decades benefits our mind, soul, and body.

The next two sentences from point 5 read "The real benefit of humor, however, is cumulative. Finding humor in everyday life over the course of decades benefits our mind, soul, and body. Unfortunately, many adults suffer from terminal seriousness. Childhood play is replaced with grumpiness, sarcasm, and mean-spirited jabs." I am often amazed at how joyless and sour so many Christians can be. I have spoken at church-related events and told funny stories, and some people are laughing so hard they are crying, while there are few others in the crowd who sit stern faced and with their arms crossed. Several years ago, after I spoke, I had a somewhat elderly man say, "You shouldn't say things to make people laugh. Church is a place for reverence and respect." When he said that, I was immediately hurt in my soul; I was hurt for him. This is a man who is considered a well-respected leader in the church, and yet he has such a poor understanding of God and the fullness of life in Christ. He is missing so much, and his understanding of the Word is so shortsighted. While I do believe church should not be a constant stand-up comedy club, there is a real need for joy and laughter to be associated with our worship. So much of God is pure joy.

Do you believe the fruits of the Spirit are in order of importance? If so, love is first, and joy is second. The fruits of the Spirit, the fruits of God, are love…and joy and…

We tell jokes and amusing stories because we like to laugh. And what is even more enjoyable is when you can share the satisfaction of laughter with a lot of people. Blessed is the person who laughs till they cry.

Have you ever noticed that *laughter* is worldwide and the same in any language? Laughter and crying are the only emotions and sounds that are made and understood by every single person on the planet. These two emotions that reach both ends of the spectrum are universal.

Why would God make something like laughter universal? Is it because he wants happiness and joy to be universal? I believe so. But it is interesting that joy and happiness are very different things.

Have you ever noticed that it never says in the Bible that God wants us to be happy? It does however mention many times that we are to be people of joy. There is a vast difference between "being happy" and "being joyful." Joy far surpasses happiness.

If repetition of words is important, consider the following. The term "fear not" (or derivations thereof) is used more than 360 times in the Bible. The word "joy" (or derivations of joy) is used over 200 times. Does it not seem obvious that God wants people to be courageous and joyful, rather than bound by fear and sorrow?

Craig Groeschel, pastor of Life.Church in Edmond, Oklahoma, once described it this way:

Happiness depends on happenings, what life is like around you. Joy is based on the presence of God. Happiness depends on what is around me, what do I have, do I have what I want? In turn, happiness can be taken away when things are taken away; when circumstances change into something we don't like. This makes us unhappy. Joy on the other hand is all about God. It is all about realizing that you have a relationship with God that far outweighs things. Things may be taken away, but joy still remains.

The question then arises, "Do we really even know what 'joy' is?"

Josh Bowers of Fresh Life Church in Montana has this to say about joy and happiness: "The dictionary defines joy as a feeling of great pleasure and happiness. The Bible defines joy as, 'Your soul's satisfaction in God. Eternal, constant and never changing. Joy is also believing God is in control and God is good.'"[63] I love that definition: "Joy is your soul's satisfaction with God."

Bowers also provides these misconceptions about joy:

1. Joy is happiness… That is not true and may not be even related at all.
2. Joy is related to your circumstances… False. Joy is never more evident than when you're going through bad circumstances. When we go through the darkest times, joy shines the brightest.
3. Joy is a feeling… False. Joy is a rock; it is solid. Joy is your soul's satisfaction in God. Eternal, constant and never changing. Joy is also believing God is in control, and God is good. How many of us look to things of this world for joy? That

---

63 Bowers, Josh. "Summer Fruit. Joy to Die For" https://vimeo.com/freshlifechurch

will always ultimately disappoint when they are gone, you had a mirage based on happiness.

In a 1990 sermon, Timothy Keller described joy as a "buoyancy that comes when you are rejoicing in God."[64]

2 Corinthians 4:16–18 says:

> Therefore, we do not lose heart. Though outwardly we are wasting away, yet inwardly we are being renewed day by day. Four our light and momentary troubles are achieving for us an eternal glory that far outweighs them all. So we fix our eyes not on what is seen, but on what is unseen. For what is seen is temporary, but what is unseen is eternal.

Keller went on to say:

> Christians have a joy. It doesn't mean we are impervious to suffering, it means we are unsinkable. We are constantly getting wet and pushed down, but we don't stay down, or at least we don't sink…The buoyancy comes from a focus on the unchanging privileges we have in God. The opposite of joy is not sadness. The reason is because the Bible is constantly talking about how you can be joyful when you are sad.
>
> Happiness comes from the comfort of having things you want. Joy is a deep kind of rejoicing and assurance and security that says I've got the only thing that really matters.

---

[64] Keller, Timothy. "Peace—Overcoming Anxiety." 2-18-1990

1 Thessalonians 4:13 says, "Brothers, we do not want you to be ignorant about those who fall asleep, or to grieve like the rest of men, who have no hope."

> The opposite of joy is not sadness, it is hopelessness. It is having nothing to really rest in.
>
> The counterfeit of joy is happiness which rests in the feeling of comfort or pleasure, it is resting in the blessings and not the blessor. To rejoice in the blessor means that you can enjoy pleasure. You can enjoy good food. You can enjoy comfort, you can enjoy physical pleasures, but you know what they are there for. They are simply little samples, like at the grocery store, not like the great food that will come out of a restaurant. Even the great physical pleasures are just those kinds of dim hints.
>
> A Christian should know more about joy than anyone else. A Christian should be able to enjoy things of this earth with the realization that this is just a preview of much greater things to come. What we experience is just a dim reflection of what will be.

"A preview of greater things to come." Can you imagine the frustration Jesus had when trying to explain the glory of heaven to his disciples? How many times must he have said, "I just can't put into words how beautiful and joyful it is. It's indescribable"?

In the early 1990s, a co-worker and I went to one of the large box bulk stores for inexpensive and quick lunch of a hot dog, pretzel, and soft drink. As we were just about to leave, we heard a blood-curling scream. "My baby! Where's my baby?" The high-pitched scream startled everyone in the store. It got louder. "Shut the doors! Shut the doors!"

It was a scream unlike anything I had ever heard before or since. We turned and saw a woman frantically running toward the front of the store, and she continued to scream, "My baby! Where's my baby?" I realize "frantic" is such an unfulfilling description of her demeanor.

The store manager and workers ran and quickly closed the large doors so nobody could leave. The woman was crazily running around looking at people and in their carts, to see who had taken her baby—screaming, crying, searching. Her adrenaline-filled heart was about to explode.

Startled, everyone started to look around. As our eyes caught the eyes of others, there were the shared expressions of sorrow, fear, and wanting to help, yet feeling helpless because we didn't know what her baby looked like or which babies belonged to which people.

After several minutes of panic and searching, someone heard a soft cry coming from a stack of tires close to the front of the store. It appeared the kidnapper got scared and hid the baby in a stack of tires before acting like an innocent fellow shopper. A few seconds and a few feet more and the kidnapper would have made it out of the store. An urgent and joyful call went out to the mother, and she ran to her child.

How do you describe the purest form of joy? I have thought about this for many years and am convinced even the greatest word-smith could not adequately describe the scene when the child was back in the arms of its mother. It is an indescribable joy.

We had two sets of friends at church who were told their sons had cancer. One was a high school senior who had been experiencing pain in his leg since he had incurred a hard block to his thigh early in the football season. When the season was over, he went to the doctor and was told he had a rare and very aggressive form of bone cancer in his left femur. The doctors were honest with the family about the unencouraging prognosis. He was immediately admitted to the hospital, and a long journey of chemotherapy and other painful treatments began. Doctors considered amputating the leg.

The other family had a two-year-old son whom they knew was in pain, but he obviously could not tell them what or where. Tests were run, and the family was told he had cancer in his spinal cord.

The shock and sadness were overwhelming. He too began the painful process of chemotherapy.

Two families. Two diagnoses of cancer in their sons. Lives suddenly being lived in hospitals. Prayers and pleadings for healing constantly being lofted high to the Father. Fatigue. Lack of sleep. Lack of appetite. Weariness from stress and sorrow. Desperation. The boys were in severe pain and discomfort. Days turned into weeks and weeks into months. Finally, both boys were declared cancer-free. Praise be to God and the many doctors and nurses who offered care.

Around this same time, I was preparing a sermon about "joy," and I independently went to both moms and asked what it was like when the doctors declared their children cancer-free. Their reactions were remarkably similar. They both thought for a moment before speaking. They began to talk, stopped, choked back tears, and finally said, "It's indescribable." How do you describe the joy when you thought your son was lost, but now he's safe or fine or found?

I think of these two mothers at church and the mother at the store. I see pure joy.

When I read the parables of Jesus with the lost sheep,[65] lost coin,[66] and prodigal son,[67] I think of these mothers and their indescribable joy. When I witness a baptism and think about the angels rejoicing in heaven, I picture the mother hugging and kissing her child as she crumples to her knees next to a stack of tires. Pure joy. Indescribable.

Just as joy can be indescribable, so can pain and sorrow. It may be in the form of cancer or another tragedy of life that crushes the body, mind, and soul. I try to imagine what Jesus felt as he was praying in the garden, betrayed by a friend and facing a savagely torturous death. It is indescribable. What kept him there when the natural instinct would be to run? According to Hebrews, it was a pure and indescribable joy. "…fixing our eyes on Jesus, the pioneer and perfecter of faith. For the joy set before him he endured the cross,

---

[65] Luke 15:3–7
[66] Luke 15:8–10
[67] Luke 15:11–32

scorning its shame, and sat down at the right hand of the throne of God."[68] It was for the joy set before him he endured the cross. As mere humans, we cannot begin to imagine what Jesus was seeing as he concentrated on the relationships, praise, worship, love, and joy of heaven. And it was his desire to share that with us that held him on the rugged wood. Pure joy.

"Laughter is an instant vacation." There was nothing laughable at the cross, but I do believe Jesus thinking about the joy of heaven transported the eyes of his mind to somewhere other than the stench-filled mound of Golgotha. He begs us to do the same. He told Peter, "In the midst of a storm, keep your focus on me."

Can you imagine what our lives would be like if even in the midst of a storm, our minds were on vacation to a place of pure joy, a soul-filled satisfaction with God?

I pray that you are a person of heaven-focused joy and that you can laugh rather than cry.

Though you have not seen him, you love him; and even though you do not see him now, *you believe in him and are filled with an inexpressible and glorious joy,* for you are receiving the end result of your faith, the salvation of your souls.
(1 Peter 1:8–9)

A joyful heart is good medicine, but a
crushed spirit dries up the bones.
(Proverbs 17:22)

We write these things that your joy may be complete.
(1 John 1:4)

---

[68] Hebrews 12:2

Chapter 6

Blue Water

"I prefer the blue water."

Many years ago, I watched a documentary about fishermen along the east coast of the United States; and they were talking about fishing different areas of the bay, the shoreline, and the open ocean and the challenges each presented. They talked about the harbors and bays and how they were generally smooth and safe as the winds and waves were buffeted by reefs and peninsulas and other landforms. They spoke of the shorelines and different tactics used as the depths and currents varied. They spoke of the open ocean, where the winds and waves can be extreme and unpredictable. Of the areas they spoke about, the open ocean was certainly the most dangerous, but all fishermen know it offers the biggest financial returns.

In a gravely hoarse voice, one grizzly old veteran of the sea mumbled, "I prefer the blue water." This was the term used for the open ocean—the blue water, where the water is deep and blue.

As these men talked about fishing, they almost laughed in derision at people who fished in the safe harbors. "Amateurs," "Stay where it's safe. Stay out of our way," "Cowards"—these, along with some unmentionable names, were just a few of the descriptions of those who fished in the harbors.

But, when these men talked about the blue water, their expressions changed. They knew the challenges of fishing in the open ocean. Hard. Cold. Unpredictable. Dangerous. In a moment's notice, it can become life or death, and the inexperienced would perish in the uncontrolled blue water. As these men spoke, there was a kinship and respect between them that can only be understood by people who sail the blue water. They are a rare breed who willingly put themselves in danger for the prize of the big catch. When this old man said, "I prefer the blue water," he was actually saying, "I prefer a challenge."

The bumper sticker simply said, "26.2." Have you ever seen one? There are no words, just the number "26.2." It is quite common, but many people do not know what it means. This bumper sticker means the driver of the car has run a full 26.2-mile marathon. This sticker has been put on the car to let the world know that the driver had the guts, drive, determination, staying power, and will to train for and run a full marathon. I must admit it is quite an amazing accomplishment, and I have never had a desire to run one.

But why the bumper sticker on the car? Why do we display such accomplishments? Why do we want someone to know that we took on a challenge and beat it?

I think the answer is quite simple: We enjoy a challenge.

- We want more responsibility at work because we hate being bored with ease and repetition. And completing the challenge might lead to a promotion or raise.
- We spend years studying, reading, and writing to obtain a master's or PhD.
- We fish in the dangerous blue water because that is where the biggest fish are and the financial payoff is better.
- We take on the challenge to lose weight and get in shape.
- We lift weights and train our bodies to receive the benefits of health and the praise of others about our physiques.

When I was working in Scotland, a man named Peter was on our development team. As he lived and worked in London and our work was at St. Andrews, I would only see Peter about once every three or four weeks. As time went by, I began to notice a change in his physical appearance. He was losing weight and gaining muscle. I also noticed how his diet had changed when we went out to eat. I asked about the obvious change I was seeing in him, and he mentioned that he was training for an event called "Tough Guy Challenge." It is a yearly endurance event in England that was originally done as training for the British version of the US Navy SEALs.

Wikipedia provides the following information about the Tough Guy Challenge:

> **Tough Guy** *claims to be the world's most demanding one-day survival ordeal.*
>
> *First staged in 1987, the Tough Guy Challenge is held on a 600-acre (2.42 square km) farm*[1] *in Perton, Staffordshire, near Wolverhampton, England, and is organised by Billy Wilson (using the pseudonym "Mr. Mouse"). It has been described as "the toughest race in the world", with up to one-third of the starters failing to finish in a typical year*
>
> *After 27 stagings of the winter event, Wilson still claimed nobody had ever finished the course according to his extremely demanding rules. The race, and its summer equivalent, has suffered two fatalities during its history.*
>
> *Taking place at the end of January, often in freezing winter conditions, the Tough Guy race is staged over a course of over 9 miles (2016 about 15 kilometres). It consists of a cross-country run including many (2016 was nine) 50 metre slalom runs up and down a hill, over 6 feet deep mud and water filled ditches (resembling the Battle of the Somme), log jumps, followed by an assault course. Claimed to be tougher than any other publicly accessible worldwide, featuring over 25 obstacles through, under and over freezing water pools, over fire pits, rope bridges, nets and so on (see detail below). The organizers claim that running the course involves risking barbed wire, cuts, scrapes, burns, dehydration, hypothermia, acrophobia, claustrophobia, electric*

shocks, sprains, twists, joint dislocation and broken bones.

Although the course is adjusted each year, its features have included a 40-foot (12.2 metres) crawl through flooded underground tunnels, balancing planks across a fire pit, and a half-mile wade through chest-deep muddy water. There are many high timber towers to climb with the Brandenburg gate at 50 feet being the highest. Marshals, dressed as warriors, fire amphibious tank gun blanks and let off exploding flares and smoke bombs over the heads of competitors as they crawl under a 70-metre section of barbed wire. Until 2000, some runners took part in the event carrying heavy wooden crucifixes.

Entrants have to be 16 or older. The event regularly attracts fields of up to 5,000 competitors, many from the United States, France, Germany and various countries around the world.

Before taking part, entrants must sign a "death warrant", which acknowledges the many risks and dangers, and which the organizers claim absolves them of any legal liability in the case of injury. First aid is provided by 2 Doctors, Paramedics, Nurses, 60 First Aiders St. John Ambulance.

As Peter described the event, my natural question was "Why do you want to do that?"

He simply answered, "I just want to see if I can push myself to do it."

Peter hired a professional trainer and developed a one-year plan to get in shape for the event. Every time I saw him, he had changed. Once a self-proclaimed "out-of-shape soft ginger" (term used in England for a person with red hair), he was now becoming a sculpted athlete. I was amazed as he described in detail his incredibly strenuous workouts. But he also described how his mind and attitude was changing. He was more confident, alert, active, disciplined, and ready to face challenges. He said work was even easier as he no longer gave in to stress and anxiety.

After Peter completed the Tough Guy Challenge, he said it was the hardest and most satisfying thing he had ever done in his life; and with a slight smile, he said he would not be doing it again.

Why do we do things like this? Why do we enjoy testing ourselves and pushing ourselves to the limit? Why do we like a challenge, especially one that requires hard work, mind over matter, mentally defeating pain, training, and dedication?

Ask people who have completed a difficult challenge, and they will all say similar things: "I grew in body, mind, and spirit." "I wanted to know in my heart that I had that something in me to push beyond the limits I had previously lived under." "I wanted to prove something to myself and/or my family." "My confidence and self-esteem skyrocketed." "I'm a better person on the other side of it."

We love a good challenge.

Isn't it ironic that we love a good challenge and yet, at the same time, we prayerfully ask God to take away our hardships, trials, and tribulations? If we see the benefits to responding to challenges, why do we ask God to remove the challenges in our lives, instead of joining the fight to overcome?

While we see the 26.2 bumper stickers, have you ever seen a bumper sticker on a car that says, "Bankruptcy," "Persecuted," "Marital Problems," "Health Problems," or "Depression"? I know I haven't ever seen one.

Could it be that we only want difficulty and strife when it is our choice—when we are in control of the severity of pain and discomfort we will endure? Will I endure a challenge at work if I know there is a raise and promotion on the other side? Likely. Will I endure the pain and suffering of losing weight and working out to get into the little black dress for the twenty-year high school reunion so that I can look better than the out-of-shape ladies who don't have their act together? The truthful vain-laden answer for many would be "You bet." I may choose to go through all the physical and mental pain to train and run a marathon, but "God, don't give me health problems or financial difficulties or… God, just please make my life challenge-free and happy."

I want to be the master of my domain. I want to control my own destiny. I want to choose my challenges, and if they get too difficult, I can ease my way out. If the work at my job is too tough, I can say, "This promotion would lead to more responsibility and time away from my family which I don't want." If the diet is too difficult, I can still accomplish my mission by purchasing a full-body compression girdle and look slimmer all while trying to keep from fainting from blood loss to the brain. If training for the marathon is hard and wearisome, I can tone the training down due to a "pain in my knee" that I don't want to turn into something serious. I am in control.

Is that an American phenomenon? Is that attitude caused by our unique expectation that everything in life should go fine, everything should work as intended, everything should make me satisfied and happy, and I should always experience instant gratification? A missionary from Africa was visiting our church one Sunday, and he said, "In America, you ask God to take away all your problems and difficulties. In Africa, we ask God to give us strength to deal with them." Why the different mind-sets among believers in the same Christ?

In the *NIV*, James 1:2–4 says, "Consider it pure joy, my brothers, whenever you face trials of many kinds, because you know that the testing of your faith develops perseverance. Perseverance must finish its work so that you may be mature and complete, not lacking anything."

In *The Message* translation, the same passage reads, "Consider it a sheer gift, friends, when tests and challenges come at you from all sides. You know that under pressure, your faith-life is forced into the open and shows its true colors. So don't try to get out of anything prematurely. Let it do its work so you become more mature and well-developed, not deficient in any way."

Some scholars will say James 1 is merely talking about temptations that lead to sin and that we should be prepared to respond with scripture in our minds the way Jesus responded to Satan. Others will say it pertains to daily struggles and tests and challenges be it leading to sin, lack of hope, despair, and weariness, much like those trials and tribulations faced by Moses, Joseph, and the Apostle Paul.

This is a struggle in my life. Joy in the prospect and presence of pain and suffering simply makes no sense to the framework of the human mind. The Apostle Paul even said he sounded like a madman when he discussed the difficulties he had endured for the cause of Christ:

> ...I know I sound like a madman, but I have served him far more! I have worked harder, been put in prison more often, been whipped times without number, and faced death again and again. Five different times the Jewish leaders gave me thirty-nine lashes. Three times I was beaten with rods. Once I was stoned. Three times I was shipwrecked. Once I spent a whole night and a day adrift at sea. I have traveled on many long journeys. I have faced danger from rivers and from robbers. I have faced danger from my own people, the Jews, as well as from the Gentiles. I have faced danger in the cities, in the deserts, and on the seas. And I have faced danger from men who claim to be believers but are not. I have worked hard and long, enduring many sleep-less nights. I have been hungry and thirsty and have often gone without food. I have shivered in the cold, without enough clothing to keep me warm.[69]

Yet, this is the same Paul who said he had learned to be content in all circumstances. I go back to Josh Bowers's definition of joy and see that Paul's soul was satisfied in God. No matter the circumstance, his soul was satisfied in God, and he was joyful.

---

[69] 2 Corinthians 11:23–27 (NLT)

I think of Paul when he was sailing on the blue water, be it the actual blue water of the ocean when he was shipwrecked on Malta[70] or being flogged, beaten, and stoned or thrown in prison or hungry and cold. How, in the midst of all of this pain and suffering, did Paul stay confident and joyful? How, after being stripped naked, severely beaten and flogged, and shackled and thrown deep into the inner cells of the prison, were Paul and Silas able to joyfully pray and sing hymns to God?[71] Why was his soul satisfied in God?

He gave us several keys:

- *Paul writes that God is faithful.*

   God will do this, for he is faithful to do what he says, and he has invited you into partnership with his Son, Jesus Christ our Lord[72]

- *Paul writes that God is trustworthy.*

   That is why I am suffering here in prison. But I am not ashamed of it, for I know the one in whom I trust, and I am sure that he is able to guard what I have entrusted to him until the day of his return.[73]

- *Paul writes that God makes us victorious.*

   And we know that in all things God works for the good of those who love him, who have been called according to his purpose.[74]

---

[70] Acts 27, 28
[71] Acts 16:22–25
[72] 1 Corinthians 11:9
[73] 2 Timothy 1:12
[74] Romans 8:28

What then shall we say in response to this? If God is for us, who can be against us? He who did not spare his own Son, but gave him up for all— how will he not also, along with him, graciously give us all things?[75]

Who shall separate us from the love of Christ? Shall trouble or hardship or persecution or famine or nakedness or danger or sword? As it is written:

"For your sake we face death all day long;
we are considered as sheep being led to be slaughtered."

No, in all things we are more than conquerors through him who loved us. For I am convinced that neither death nor life, neither angels or demons, neither the present nor the future, nor any powers, neither height nor depth, nor anything else in all creation, will be able to separate us from the love of God that is in Christ Jesus our Lord.[76]

- *Paul is familiar with the ancient scriptures and knows God wants what is best for us.*

This is what the Lord says: "You will be in Babylon for seventy years. But then I will come and do for you all the good things I have promised, and I will bring you home again. For I know the plans I have for you," says the Lord. "They are plans for good and not for disaster, to give you a future and a hope. In those days when you pray, I will listen. If you look for me wholeheart-

---

[75] Romans 8:31–32
[76] Romans 8:35–38

edly, you will find me. I will be found by you,"
says the Lord.[77]

John and Lisa Pickens endured the agony of watching their
daughter battle and succumb to a rare form of cancer. I often think
of a question he asked while facing such a difficult challenge of life,
"How do I come out on the other side?" The truth is the challenges
we face will eventually come to an end. Some will be resolved on this
side of life, while others end at our death. Regardless, the question
remains the same, "How do I come out on the other side of this?"

There seems to be two options:

1. *Give in to misery and despair.*

While in college, I mowed yards for extra money. Every
Thursday, I mowed a yard for an elderly lady who was an absolute
joy. Each time I would go to collect my pay, she was happy, cheerful,
and thankful. One day, she came to the door, and it was easy to tell
she had been crying; and she informed me she had just been diagnosed with cancer. I tried my best to console her, but my youth and
inexperience in life was glaring. The following week, I mowed her
yard and knocked on the door, only to be met by a bearded man I
guessed was in his late thirties. He sorrowfully said his mother had
died earlier in the week. In eleven days, she had gone from being a
happy and cheerful woman to dead and lying in a coffin. I know
there are some cancers that can kill very quickly, but I have always
wondered if the news of her cancer simply crushed her spirit to the
point of completely giving up on life.

2. *Fight the good fight.*

I am reminded of the battle with cancer that my mother-in-law
endured. What started as bladder cancer eventually spread into the
lungs. While cancer is not a fair fight, Nana always kept a smile on

---

[77] Jeremiah 29:10–14

her face. She explicitly instructed everyone in the family that when they were at the hospital with her, they were always to be polite, cheerful, and thankful to anyone they came in contact with, be it a doctor, nurse, or janitor. As the fight progressed, she developed the attitude saying, "Either way, I win. If I beat cancer and get to stay on earth with my family, I win. If I pass away and get to be with 'my Jesus,' I win." Her soul was satisfied with God. Nana won and got to see "her Jesus" when she was sixty-six years old.

Paul was in prison in Rome. He too was approximately sixty-six years old and knew he was likely not going to make it out alive. While writing a second letter to his friend and companion, Timothy, he penned these famous words:

> For I am already poured out like a drink offering, and the time has come for my departure. I have fought the good fight, I have finished the race, I have kept the faith. Now, there is in store for me the crown of righteousness, which the Lord, the righteous Judge, will award to me on that day—and not only me, but also to all who have longed for his appearing.[78]

His journey as history's most successful Christian evangelist was filled with immense joy, relationships, love, and higher accomplishments. But he had also endured harsh persecution, excruciating beatings, and unjust imprisonments. Almost as if he was openly asking the personal question to Timothy, "How will I come out on the other side of this?" his answer was clear: "I will be handed a crown. I win. Either way, I win."

Enjoy the blue water.

---

[78] 2 Timothy 4:6–8

Chapter 7

Anonymous

What was the widow's name?

When I had consistent work, April and I tried to be very generous with our money. We supported various causes, helped fundraisers at Celina schools, and supported charities and ministries. We also bought Walmart and grocery store gift cards which we anonymously mailed to people we knew were in need.

After my golf course work dried up, things had gotten very tight financially. As our goal was simply to make it through each day, donating money and offering gifts was extremely difficult.

The budget crunch was hard on everyone, but I was always sensitive to the kids. They were stuck in the middle of our struggle, and I wondered if they understood what was happening and why. I wondered if they were embarrassed or upset. If so, they never mentioned it, even at Christmas when each child got only a package of socks, a package of underwear, and a package of gum.

It was becoming evident we were going to lose the house and land if things did not change soon. I was experiencing another one of those days where I couldn't figure out what to do and didn't know who else to call for work. I was bored, so I walked to the mailbox, not looking for anything in particular. The house was in the middle of the forty acres, so the walk to the mailbox was just under one thousand feet. I got there and found some bills, advertisements, and a small white envelope with no return address. The bills were no surprise as they were ever-present. The advertisements were trash because we couldn't afford anything. The small envelope was odd, as our names were written on the front, but there was no return address. I opened it and found five one hundred-dollar Walmart gift cards wrapped in a plain white piece of paper with no writing on it. It was anonymous.

For a moment, I stood and looked at the cards and then began to sob uncontrollably. We were in desperate need, but I was overcome with shame and embarrassment. How had it come to this? I was the one who sent out these cards. I was not the one who would receive them. My humiliation was complete.

I began the long walk back to the house consumed in thought that I was now receiving pity from strangers. After a couple hundred yards, I stopped and looked again at the gift cards. My shame was again overwhelming, but for a different reason. I held the cards and thought, *You jerk! You arrogant idiot! Someone is trying to help your family, and your pride is causing you to be upset. Someone has done exactly what you've been doing for years, and now you're on the receiving end, and you're embarrassed.* I again began to sob, but this time out of disgust with myself. How had I let pride become such a destructive presence in my life?

I had often read about pride in the Bible, but figured it was a warning for someone else, right? The irony of that thought is stifling.

While considering pride and arrogance, I found myself going to the writings of Solomon, one who knew firsthand the negative effects of pride and self-centeredness:

> There are six things the Lord hates; Indeed seven are repulsive to Him: A proud look [the attitude that makes one overestimate oneself and discount others], a lying tongue, And hands that shed innocent blood, A heart that creates wicked plans, Feet that run swiftly to evil, A false witness who breathes out lies [even half-truths], And one who spreads discord (rumors) among brothers.[79]

---

[79] Proverbs 6:16–18 (Amplified Bible)

The [reverent] fear and worship awe of the Lord includes the hatred of evil; Pride and arrogance and the evil way, And the perverted mouth, I hate.[80]

Pride goes before destruction, And a haughty spirit before a fall.[81]

"Why does God hate pride so much?" For this answer, I turn to two men wiser than me.

First, in his message "Hope for a Doomed Nation," John Macarthur says:

God hates pride. He hates haughty eyes. It destroys love. It destroys relationships, all of them. What is the killer of all relationships? Pride. Pride kills all relationships. It kills care, it kills sacrifice, it kills kindness. It kills the supreme virtue of all virtues: humility.

Second, in *Mere Christianity*, C. S. Lewis says, "As long as you are proud you cannot know God. A proud man is always looking down on things and people: and, of course, as long as you are looking down you cannot see something that is above you."

Further in his writing, Lewis goes on to say:

The vice I am talking of is Pride or Self-Conceit: and the virtue opposite to it, in Christian morals, is called Humility. You may remember, when I was talking about sexual morality, I warned you that the centre of Christian morals did not lie there. Well, now, we have come to the centre. According to Christian teachers, the essential vice, the utmost evil, is Pride. Unchastity, anger,

---

[80] Proverbs 8:13 (AMP)
[81] Proverbs 16:18 (AMP)

greed, drunkenness, and all that, are mere flea-bites in comparison: it was through Pride that the devil became the devil: Pride leads to every other vice: it is the complete anti-God state of mind. Does this seem to you exaggerated? If so, think it over. I pointed out a moment ago that the more pride one had, the more one disliked pride in others. In fact, if you want to find out how proud you are the easiest way is to ask yourself, "How much do I dislike it when other people snub me, or refuse to take any notice of me, or shove their oar in, or patronise me, or show off?" The point is that each person's pride is in competition with everyone else's pride. It is because I wanted to be the big noise at the party that I am so annoyed at someone else being the big noise. Two of a trade never agree. Now what you want to get clear is that Pride is essentially competitive—is competitive by its very nature—while the other vices are competitive only, so to speak, by accident. Pride gets no pleasure out of having something, only out of having more of it than the next man. We say that people are proud of being rich, or clever, or good-looking, but they are not. They are proud of being richer, or cleverer, or better-looking than others. If everyone else became equally rich, or clever, or good-looking there would be nothing to be proud about. It is the comparison that makes you proud: the pleasure of being above the rest. Once the element of competition has gone, pride has gone.[82]

---

[82] C. S. Lewis, *Mere Christianity* (New York: Simon & Schuster Touchstone edition, 1996), 109

I am amazed at that line, "…it was through Pride that the devil became the devil: Pride leads to every other vice: it is the complete anti-God state of mind." This is consistent with Saint Augustine saying, "It was pride that changed angels into devils; it is humility that makes men as angels."

Standing and crying at the mailbox, my first thought was the gift symbolized my failing and inability to care for my family. As I walked back to the house, the reality hit me hard that my problem wasn't feelings of failure, but rather my enormous pride was under attack. I think again of the C. S. Lewis line, "The point is that each person's pride is in competition with everyone else's pride. It is because I wanted to be the big noise at the party that I am so annoyed at someone else being the big noise." I ask myself, "Was my hurt because I was no longer the big noise? Was my hurt because someone had wrestled away my coveted title of 'giver'?" My pride had created an enormous chasm between me and God.

That day was a wake-up call. Not only had my pride became evident in my inability to receive well but I also needed to evaluate my attitude in giving. In giving, I had to ask, "Was my heart right? And who was on the receiving end?"

When April and I anonymously gave gift cards, I always assumed those on the receiving end would be overcome with joy. In my mind, I thought the recipients would imagine a muscular and ruggedly handsome man with long blond flowing hair sitting shirtless on an unsaddled white Arabian stallion on a white-sanded beach. Sitting behind him was his beautiful tanned wife in a bikini, and they were both staring over the distant waves of the ocean as the orange setting sun created a soft glow on their faces. With that picture in mind, I figured the recipients would be overcome with gratitude. As I couldn't relate, I had never fully thought about the mental struggles of someone in need.

I began to examine my heart when it came to giving. Why was I doing it? What was I trying to accomplish? Was my gift out of genuine love for people, or was it to make me feel better and justify my own financial success? Was my giving born of a desire for others to see my grand generosity? Was it all about me rather than being about love and compassion for my neighbor? Was I following the greatest commandment at all?

Mark 12 offers a story on giving that is life changing. I must admit this passage impacted me partly because of the notes in my *NIV Study Bible*. I have said I am not a Bible scholar or great theologian and I need help in understanding scripture. So, in addition to Bible-based websites, handbooks, and commentaries, I often refer to notes at the bottom of my Bible that will educate and lead me to different areas of study and knowledge.

I believe every word is in the Bible for a reason, and there are times when God will reveal things that are incredibly significant that have been hiding in plain sight under our noses for a lifetime. Welcome to Mark 12:

> And one of the teachers of the law came and heard them debating. Noticing that Jesus had given them a good answer, he asked him, "Of all the commandments, which is the most important?
>
> "The most important one," answered Jesus, "is this: 'Hear, O Israel, the Lord our God, the Lord is one. Love the Lord your God with all your heart and with all your soul and with all your strength.' The second is this: 'Love your neighbor as yourself.' There is no commandment greater than these."[83]
>
> While Jesus was teaching in the temple courts,[84]… The large crowd listened to him with delight. As he taught, Jesus said, "Watch out for the teachers of the law. They like to walk around in flowing robes and be greeted in the marketplaces, and have the most important seats in the synagogues and the places of honor at banquets. They devour widows' houses and for show make

---

[83] Mark 12:28–31 (NIV)
[84] Mark 12:35 (NIV)

lengthy prayers. Such men will be punished most severely." Jesus sat down opposite the place where the offerings were put and watched the crowd putting their money into the temple treasury. Many rich people threw in large amounts. But a poor widow woman came and put in two very small copper coins, worth only a fraction of a penny. Calling His disciples to him, Jesus said, "I tell you the truth, this poor widow has put in more into the treasury than all the others. They all gave out of their wealth; but she, out of her poverty, put in everything—all she had to live on."[85]

I intentionally transcribed this different from as it appears in the Bible. The *NIV Study Bible* includes headings and text separations that I believe are detrimental to understanding this text. Removing the separations allows the text to flow.

Jesus just taught that the greatest commands are to love God and love your neighbor as yourself. He then began teaching in the temple courts about the hypocrisy and evil doings of the "teachers of the law," comparing them to the poor widow who humbly put two small coins in the treasury.

I believe there are four significant aspects of this story:

1. The use of the words "threw" and "put." The text says, "Many rich people *threw* in large amounts. But a poor widow woman came and *put* in two very small copper coins." As I said before, I believe every word is in the Bible for a reason. Why does the Bible specifically differentiate between the words "threw" and "put"?

2. In the *NIV Study Bible* notes for Mark 12:41, it says, "Located in the court of the women. Both men and women

---

[85] Mark 12:37–44

were allowed in this court, but women could go no farther into the temple buildings. It contained 13 trumpet-shaped receptacles for contributions brought by worshipers." The rich would come in with their flowing robes and intentionally create a scene and generate noise as they "threw" their money into the receptacles, or "shopheroth." The more they gave, the increased noise would generate the attention they craved. Can you imagine the sound created if these receptacles were metal and the rich people were literally throwing their copper coins? Remember the C. S. Lewis line about who can be the biggest noise at the party. I wonder, *If the rich were giving the equivalent of one dollar, would they throw the minimal four quarters or instead throw twenty nickels to make more noise?*

The text says the widow "put" her contribution into the receptacle. She did not make a scene. She did not desire attention. Simply wanting to serve the Lord in genuine humility, she gently put her two coins in the bottom of the receptacle.

3. The widow gave all she had. It is one thing to be wealthy and give some; there is often no pain or anxiety involved. It is just some of much. But, when you are poor and you give all you have, that is pure—pure faith, pure trust, pure hope. She is the pure embodiment of the greatest commands that Jesus has just described in verses 29–31.

4. The title separating verses 40 and 41 reads "The Widow's Offering." I intentionally removed this, because the break can make the reader think the following text is a different time and place, which is detrimental in this text. In verse 40, Jesus had just spoken about the rich and how "They devour widows' houses." The very next verse tells a story about one of these widows and how she was walking into the temple and making her donation in the midst of the rich people who might be the very ones who had taken,

or devoured, all her possessions. These rich people in their flowing robes might be the exact reason she was poor and had only "two very small copper coins."

The rich were doing all they could to draw attention to themselves. They might even be using money they took from this poor widow to elevate themselves. She humbly and quietly walked in. She did not yell at them or make loud accusations of robbery. She did not scowl or show displeasure or anger. Likely with her head down, she might even have to occasionally pause or stop to keep from bumping into the rich as they hurriedly moved around the room as they put on their show of self-glorification. She simply walked in and quietly made an offering of pure love and worship. I wish I knew whether or not she said a quiet prayer of praise and thankfulness as she put the coins in the receptacle. She gave all she had. Then she left. I wonder where she went after she left the temple.

Could James, the half brother of Jesus, have been thinking about this woman when he wrote James 4:6 which says, "...God opposes the proud, but gives grace to the humble"?[86]

As I read about this woman, I consider my life and my giving. I wish I could say my giving was like the widow, but I'm afraid I trended toward the rich givers. We had money, and it was no great sacrifice to give. We wanted to help, but in my case, I don't remember it ever flowing from a deeply humble and sincere heart. Could it be that God needed to teach me some lessons about love and pride and humility?

I went from being wealthy to completely financially broke. But even in that broke condition, my pride was killing me. It took an anonymous gift to open my eyes and highlight my extreme pride and ego.

---

[86] James 4:6

We still struggle financially, and I relate more and more to the widow. Giving money is hard, so sometimes the only way we can help is with time and physical labor. When we are able to give financially, I try to look at it from the standpoint of the widow woman. I pray that I have the love and care that she showed. I pray for God to touch my heart and make it pure.

The next part of this journey is considering the person on the receiving end. I specifically think about the person who is weary and at the end of their rope. They may be in a position they have never been before; and they are emotionally, physically, and spiritually spent. They are trying as hard as they can to make things work; and everything they have done successfully in the past, for some reason, is simply not working now. They are used to being able to do things on their own to care for themselves and their families. They receive a gift, and as odd as it sounds, it feels like the final nail in the coffin. I would have never understood that feeling if I had not stood at a mailbox and felt that sting.

Before my mailbox experience, not once did I ever think someone would be embarrassed or hurt. Never did it cross my mind that there could be a man who would receive a gift and feel like it was a sign that he was not able to provide for his family.

I received an anonymous letter in the mail, and I was now walking in the other person's shoes. For the first time, I was on the receiving end, and the picture was quite different. I too saw someone trying to do a kindness, but my pride had turned their kindness into my embarrassment. It completely changed my point of view about giving, receiving, and pride.

As hard as it is, I hope everyone understands there are simply some times in your life when you need help. But we are conditioned that the American way is to be a rugged individual. The Marlboro Man, sitting on his horse all alone in the wild countryside, a look of steely determination on his timeworn face, needs no help. He can do it himself. That idea of pride and individualism can cloud our minds, especially among the family of believers. I think of Acts 4:32–37 where the new Christians were selling all they had and giving to the poor and needy of the group. That is family and community and loving your neighbor.

Pride is such a difficult thing. Some pride is good, such as taking pride in your work and making sure you do things right. But when pride is all about elevating yourself, a great chasm is created between yourself and God.

Have you ever been in our situation? Broke and feeling like you have no value? I am struck by this story and Jesus's ability to use this woman's poverty and humility to touch the lives of every person who has ever read a Bible. How many millions of people have read of this humble woman who gave all she had and never asked for anything in return? I wonder, *Did her age ever allow her to hear the eventual writings of the Book of Mark and realize she had been written about?* By her example, I am reminded that when we are humble, God can use us in every phase of our lives, in weakness and strength, wealth and poverty. His grace is sufficient.

As I write this, we are still financially poor and struggling every day to make ends meet. But there are times April and I see a need that we feel we must participate in, even though our contribution may be very small. When I now give, I offer a quick prayer:

> *Lord God, please touch my heart and help me to understand your love for all people. Please help me to be humble and always thankful.*
>
> *Lord, please help this person to receive this offering in the manner it is intended. Please help them know it is given with a heart of love and understanding. Please help the person who receives this to not feel ashamed or embarrassed, but to see the glory of a loving God being played out through the hands of a humble sinner. If this person is struggling with pride, please heal them and bring them the full measure of your joy.*

I offer a quick prayer for you:

> *I pray that you are truly humble and love God. I pray that you are a generous and giving person. I pray that you feel his pure joy. I pray that you recognize and defeat destructive pride in your life and walk humbly with God. And I pray God will bless your two copper coins...whether you are giving them or receiving them.*

To this day I do not know who sent us those gift cards. Just as the name of the widow woman is never given, they are...

anonymous.

Chapter 8

A Choice

Golfweek, March 11, 2006.

How can a simple golf publication have such an impact on my life?

It was the annual issue ranking "America's Best 100 Golf Courses." As a golf course architect, this is a very important publication as it can significantly upgrade your marketing if one of your courses makes the list. I opened the magazine and ignored all other articles and advertisements until I found the list for the Top 100 Modern Courses (1960–present) and began looking for any familiar names. There it was.

67. (NR) Whisper Rock Golf Club (Lower)* (p)
Scottsdale, Arizona
Phil Mickelson and Gary Stephenson, 2001

The (NR) and "*" both stand for "not previously ranked," while the (p) means the course is private. For a five-year-old golf course to be ranked this high is quite an honor considering the thousands of golf courses built in the United States between 1960 and 2006.

After a moment of satisfaction, I turned back to the magazine's front cover which was highlighting my favorite course, Cypress Point Golf Club, in Pebble Beach, California. Built by Alister MacKenzie in 1928 on the cliffs of the Pacific Ocean, this is one of the most beautiful and iconic golf courses in the world. Ranked as the number

1 golf course in America, there is almost a spiritual feeling as you walk those hallowed grounds.

I turned to the article and was somewhat surprised as I immediately recognized a man I had seen the previous year on a trip to Cypress Point. When I saw him in 2005, I didn't know who he was, but I did think it peculiar that a man with a limp right arm would be in the pro shop at this prestigious course. He was unassuming and quiet, but he had an air of humility and dignity about him that caught my attention. He was wearing a Cypress Point golf shirt, and the way he moved with familiarity around the shop and grounds made me believe he was one of the pro shop workers. Looking at the magazine, I thought, *Why would* Golfweek *have a picture of a pro shop worker take up two full pages of their magazine?* It wasn't until I started reading that I discovered his name was Jim Langley, and he was a little more than a worker in the shop; he was the Head Golf Professional at Cypress Point. In fact, "in 1971, he became only the third Head Professional in the history of the Cypress Point Golf Club."[87] I had no idea he was a legend in the world of golf, and this article was written to honor him as he had recently retired in 2005.

Written by John Steinbreder, the article was titled "INSPIRED PAIRING, Langley and Cypress Point: Spiritual man at a soulful place." Steinbreder told the story of the 1971 retirement of Henry Puget, who had been the Head Golf Professional at Cypress Point since 1931.

> *Almost on a whim, Langley submitted a resume and application for the job. The interview process entailed perhaps a half-dozen meetings—and rounds of golf—with club officials. The Cypress president Charles de Bretteville called the man who had never been a head pro anywhere and worked only half a year at any sort of golf operation and said, "Langley, I am going to take a chance on you."*[88]

---

[87] Steinbreder, John. "INSPIRED PAIRING, Langley and Cypress Point: Spiritual man at a soulful place." *Golfweek* (March 11, 2006): 16–20

[88] Steinbreder, "INSPIRED PAIRING." 20

And with that, Jim Langley, a man with no experience at all, was named head golf professional at one of the most prestigious golf clubs in the world. From the outside looking in, this makes absolutely no sense. But the officials at Cypress Point recognized something special in Jim.

The article told of Jim's work at the club and "servicing a membership roll that had its share of celebrities, business moguls and political leaders."[89] By all accounts, Jim was doing an exceptional job in his new role and also enjoyed playing golf, even carding the course record of 63 in the summer of 1978.

The following is an excerpt of a day that changed many lives:

> *Things came crashing down in fall 1987. That's when Langley was driving former club president Bill Borland to a pro-am match at the San Francisco Golf Club late one afternoon. A faulty fuel gauge caused them to run out of gas, and Langley got out to push the car in the dark with Borland at the wheel. Just as they arrived at the next exit ramp, they were struck by another auto that was traveling more than 50 mph. The impact momentarily trapped Langley's legs between both cars' bumpers and then threw him off the side of the road.*
>
> *"I just remember waking up in the hospital," Langley recalls. "My legs were broken and swollen to four or five times their normal size. I didn't think much about my arm, but I learned later on I had pretty extensive nerve damage there."*
>
> *Langley spent two months in a Bay Area hospital and a spell in a New Orleans facility, where doctors tried unsuccessfully to restore some function to his right arm through a nerve-grafting procedure. It was nearly a year before he was able to go back to work.*[90]

---

89 Steinbreder, "INSPIRED PAIRING." 20
90 Steinbreder, "INSPIRED PAIRING." 20

I went back to the beginning of the article and reread the opening paragraphs:

> *Jim Langley says he is the luckiest guy in the world, and in many ways it is easy to understand why he feels that way.*
>
> *But sometimes you have to wonder what the 6-foot-4 Langley is talking about. His legs throb in constant pain, as a result of a 1987 car accident that led to more than a dozen operations. His right arm, the one he calls his "quiet partner," was rendered all but useless after that crash, meaning he has been relegated to playing one-handed since.*
>
> *Oh, and then there was the sense of vulnerability and humiliation that came in the wake of his near-death experience.*
>
> *"I worried I had lost some of my manhood," Langley recalls. "Here I am, with only one good arm and two bad legs, wondering how I can protect my wife and children."*
>
> *But even as he recalls that gut-wrenching emotion, Langley is quick to reaffirm his belief in his good fortune.*
>
> *"I'm lucky in that the accident made me appreciate each day, and the many great things in my life," he says. "It also gave me a chance to make a positive example and show you can overcome things. I have never asked, 'Why me?' In fact, I have always felt I was better equipped to handle something like this than most because I have my faith and family, and because I have Cypress Point."*[91]

---

[91] Steinbreder, "INSPIRED PAIRING." 17

Jim Langley in the
early 1970's

After the accident. Playing
golf with one arm.
(Photo by Marcia LaRosa)

This was the man I saw in the golf pro shop, a tall lean man with a limp right arm—quiet, unassuming, humble, gracious. I did not know him when he was a basketball player at the University of California at Berkeley. I did not know him when he was a United States Marine or afterward when he worked at International Paper selling corrugated boxes. I did not know him when he briefly played on the PGA Tour or, when that didn't work out, when he became a school teacher. I didn't know him when he moved his family back to Salinas, California, and went to work loading lettuce onto trucks and cauliflower onto train cars.

I wonder, *Was it during one of his breaks loading lettuce that he read the newspaper and noticed a story about Henry Puget retiring from Cypress Point that led him to apply for the job?* An application that might have been the most titanic long shot of all time. Think about it. While preparing his resume for one of the most prestigious jobs in the world, under "Most Recent Job Experience," Jim would have listed "lettuce loader."

Club insiders have long averred that Langley initially received the head pro job because his stout character elevated him above all other candidates. And that attribute only seemed to be more apparent when he came back. "It's as if he grew even further in stature as a result of his tragedy," says Dr. Tom Loss, a Seattle dentist and U.S. Golf Association rules official who is a Cypress member. "Being around Jim was like going to church; he was that good and inspiring a person."

It is interesting to hear those references to religion because Jim Langley truly is a spiritual man. He developed that in his youth, thanks mostly to his mother, who sneaked her children into the local Catholic church on Sundays despite the fierce opposition of her Southern Baptist husband, who didn't attend the weddings of any of his children because they all took place in Catholic places of worship. And not surprisingly, his devotion grew stronger in the years after his accident, as he had to dig deep to persevere in a world that suddenly had turned very cruel.

Men and women of faith often seek solace in places of quiet beauty, and Jim Langley took walks on Cypress Point almost every afternoon he worked there, sometimes carrying a short iron or maybe fondling a rosary in his pocket. He ambled along fairways and over dunes. He stood at oceanside promontories and listened to the sea lions bark. He said prayers for his friends and after the accident gave thanks for what Langley calls his second chance.

He also asked for the wisdom to know how to be a better person, and to be a blessing to others in the way they have been to him. And whenever he got to the 15th tee, he dropped a single golf ball into the ravine there, in memory of an old caddie and friend who died five years ago (and delighted in finding balls in that spot).

Today, Langley takes these walks as a Cypress member. And he continues to stop at many of the same spots, to say prayers and to give thanks.

But those who know Jim Langley say they are the ones who should be giving thanks—for his enduring compassion and deep humility, and for teaching them things that are far more important than how to hit a 3-iron.[92]
(Special thanks to John Steinbreder)

When I first read this article in March of 2006, our lives had leveled out. I had several golf design jobs, and we were not in financial need. And we had not yet learned of the cancer that would befall April's mother and the eventual impact that would have on our lives.

I thought the article was interesting and inspiring. But, as strange as it may sound, at that time, I was not in need of an inspirational story. Everything was fine, no worries. Life was good.

However, I admit something was nagging at me. Why did I remember this man so well? I had only seen him for a minute or two and never spoke to him. He was just someone talking to another man in a golf shop. But, even then, there was something about him that caught my attention. The easy answer is the withered right arm that is uncommon at a sporting venue such as golf, but it was more than that. Something about him said "elegant humility." Is there even such a thing?

You may wonder how this article changed my life. After I read the magazine in 2006, I set it on a shelf in my office. Over time, papers and other magazines got stacked on top of it, and it drifted from memory. It wasn't until December of 2011 that I saw it again.

April's mother had passed away a year earlier in December of 2010. Having never dealt with the death of someone so close, we did not anticipate the lingering sadness that struck so unexpectedly

---

[92] Steinbreder, "INSPIRED PAIRING." 20

on birthdays, Mother's Day, numerous sporting events, and special holidays when her empty chair was so prominent.

In late 2011, we had our cancer scare with April. In losing the house and moving, my children were devastated to be leaving their friends, school, sports, and church. We were having continual maintenance problems with our aging cars. We had to scrimp and save every penny to buy food for the family. I had lost all of my work. My physical and mental health was faltering. My identity was gone. We were packing to leave our dream home. As much as we tried to stay faithful and Christlike, this home that had been a place of immeasurable joy was now filled with sorrow as we were loading boxes and saying goodbye to very dear friends. Broken hearts are heavy.

My faith was wavering as I struggled with God. There were times when I felt strong and courageous and knew God, in his encompassing love, was looking after us. But there were also times of anger at God for allowing this or causing this to happen. My anger wasn't so much for what was happening to me, but rather for the hurt that my wife and children were experiencing. "Why was my family being punished for my failings?" It was a spiritual roller coaster.

While packing my office, I sifted through stacks of paper and magazines trying to decide what to keep or throw away. In one dusty stack, I came across this *Golfweek* magazine and immediately remembered there was a good story about "the one-armed golf pro at Cypress." I opened the magazine and began reading. You can imagine the impact it had on me at that time. Dealing with hurt and anger, I was reading about a man who was severely injured and still had the character and faith to inspire and minister to people. There was one portion of the article that hit me particularly hard:

> *In fact, his generosity is such that men and women of even the steeliest resolve find their eyes welling with tears when they talk about Jim.*
>
> *"Jim absolutely loves people, and he has an unselfish concern for them that moves us all," says Cypress member Sam Reeves, his voice cracking slightly as he speaks. "He also has a life of joy, which*

is remarkable when you think of what he has gone through. Joy, you understand, is different from happiness. Joy is an inward peace, a sense of contentment and acceptance of life and what it gives you. And while pain may be inevitable, suffering is a choice. Jim has pain, a lot of pain, but he chooses not to suffer. Rather, he gives, and he inspires as a result.[93]

"While pain is inevitable, suffering is a choice." I read that line over and over again. "Suffering is a choice."

I believe the suffering mentioned here is different from physical suffering. Obviously, Jim Langley had physical pain which could be debilitating at times. But this suffering pertains to a mental attitude and not allowing the physical pain and its limitations to result in a life of anxiety and sorrow. In the midst of great physical pain, Jim chose not to suffer mental distress.

I am reminded of the wisdom of King Solomon as he wrote:

A cheerful heart is good medicine, but a crushed spirit dries up the bones.[94]

This is exactly what Jim Langley had tapped into—the understanding that joy and gladness can heal, but suffering can dry up the bones.

I was suffering greatly, but mine was not due to physical injury; it was emotional, psychological, and spiritual. My mental suffering was impacting my relationships with everyone around me. I was sad, quiet, and tired. My suffering had created a gulf between me and God as I kept asking, "Why?" My suffering had led to feelings of uselessness and inferiority.

I read about Jim Langley and thought to myself, *Do I have a choice in my suffering?* As much as I resented admitting it, I absolutely

---

[93] Steinbreder, "INSPIRED PAIRING." 18

[94] Proverbs 17:22

had a choice, and I was currently letting Satan win. I was not being strong and courageous.

There were many things in this short *Golfweek* paragraph that touched my soul, but there was a familiarity to Sam Reeves's words when he said "a sense of contentment." This sounded remarkably close to the words of the Apostle Paul when he wrote, "I am not saying this because I am in need, for I have learned to be content whatever the circumstances."[95] Speaking of joy and contentment the way Sam did, I wondered if he was a Christian himself and familiar with the writings of the Apostle Paul or James, the half brother of Christ.

> Consider it pure joy, my brothers, whenever you face trials of many kinds, because you know that the testing of your faith develops perseverance. Perseverance must finish its work so that you may be mature and complete, not lacking anything.[96]
>
> Blessed is the man who perseveres under trial, because when he has stood the test, he will receive the crown of life that God has promised to those who love him.[97]

I wish I could say I read this article and, as I packed my office, was immediately changed into a joyful and content person. I wasn't. My pain was deep and mixed with anger, and I wasn't able to immediately flip a switch and change. But I was well aware I had to work to defeat a suffering mind-set.

I have read that article many times since that day, and I have drawn a tremendous amount of strength from the resolve and faith of Jim Langley. It has taken time to let the message of his life sink in and to realize I have a choice about the attitude with which I live my life. I may not have a choice about some things that happen around me and to me, but I absolutely have a choice as to how I will respond.

---

[95] Philippians 4:11
[96] James 1:2–4
[97] James 1:12

Inevitably, there will be times of pain and sorrow, but I have a choice to dwell in the hollow of God's victorious hand rather the stifling cave of suffering.

A choice.

What does all of this mean? This is a great story, but what does it mean? I want to consider six takeaways:

(1) Keep reading.

I was suffering. Then, one day, I found an article in a golf publication that provided deep inspiration. I read about joy, contentment, resolve, faith, second chances, pain, humility, fear of loss, courage, prayer, walking with God, and taking a chance on someone who was unqualified and putting them in a position of great prominence.

Sound familiar?

1. Joy...................................Sarah (Genesis 21:6)
2. Contentment................Paul (Philippians 4:11)
3. Resolve..........................Stephen (Acts 7)
4. Faith...............................Abraham (Genesis 22:1–19)
5. Second Chances...........Jonah (Book of Jonah)
6. Pain................................Job (Job 1–3)
7. Humility........................David (Psalm 51)
8. Fear of loss...................Rich young ruler (Mark 10:17–22)
9. Courage.........................Joshua (Joshua 1:9)
10. Prayer.............................Isaiah (Isaiah 64)
11. Walk with God..............Adam (Genesis 3:8)
12. Use of unqualified.......Moses (Exodus 3:1–4:17)

All of the inspirational aspects of Jim Langley's story are found in the Bible. There is strength and hope in the inspired Word of God. And, just like I did with the *Golfweek* story, we need to read the biblical accounts over and over again until they resonate and impact our lives.

(2) Your impact.

I found great inspiration reading about a humble man in *Golfweek* magazine. He did not set out to live a life calculated to draw attention to himself. In the midst of great pain, he did not wallow in sorrow and self-pity, even though it would have been justified by society. He did not boast in his position of prominence or in what he was accomplishing. He simply lived a life of deep faith and joy and chose not to suffer. His impact was immeasurable, even though it was never orchestrated.

    a.   You can do the same.

Do you believe you can have a similar impact on people? You might be saying, "I've never been hit by a car and lived to tell about it." It is not the size of your tribulation that counts; it is the size of your response. Faith, obedience, and courage is contagious. Whether or not it is on a scale that compels someone to write about you in a national publication or not, you have the ability to inspire, and I believe you are called to do so.

    b.   You relate to someone.

There are many stories of courage and faith in our daily lives. This story of Jim Langley is impactful to me because I relate to him through the game of golf. I understand how unlikely it was for him to get that job and then to perform it with his eventual physical limitations. We love stories about people we can relate to as it gives us hope that we can do the same.

Who can you impact for good because they relate to you? Think of people you spend time or have something in common with. You have the ability to impact those people greatly toward the doorstep of heaven. Are you?

    c.   You never know who is watching.

Jim Langley and I never spoke. We simply crossed paths for a brief minute in a golf shop, yet there was something about him that caught my attention. Unfortunately, that encounter was soon forgotten once I got out on the course and reveled in the incredible beauty of the golf course. It wasn't until a year later that I opened a magazine, saw his picture, and read an article that I knew the measure of the man. His story has had a tremendous impact on my life, and he never knew it.

Whether you know it or not, you are impacting someone today. People are watching you, especially if you call yourself a Christian. Think of your actions today. What did you do today? Where did you go? Who did you interact with personally or from a distance such as in another car? Who did you talk to, text, or email? What was your language like today? How did you act? Question: If you were watching yourself, would you be positively or negatively impacted toward Christ?

(3) Courage.

True courage is exceedingly rare, and we are mesmerized when we see it. We dream about being people of courage and fearlessness. We love gymnast Kerri Strug who vaulted in the 1996 Olympics despite having an injured ankle. We admire Heather Dorniden when she got up after falling in her six hundred-meter race. We rightfully venerate Desmond Doss who saved seventy-five fellow soldiers at the battle of Hacksaw Ridge in World War 2 (*Hacksaw Ridge* released in 2016 based on his life). Why else do you think movies like *Gladiator, Braveheart, Unbroken, Rocky, To Kill a Mockingbird,* and *It's A Wonderful Life* are so popular? We love seeing courage, determination, and staying power. We long for it in our lives.

The same is true of the Bible. God is continually pleading for his people to have courage and not be afraid. Think of the words of Joshua 1:9:

> Have I not commanded you? Be strong and courageous. Do not be frightened, and do not be dismayed, for the Lord your God is with you wherever you go.

The inspired Word of God gives us numerous examples of courageous people: Noah, Joseph, Moses, Joshua, Rahab, Caleb, Esther,

Gideon, David, Daniel, Shadrach, Meshach, Abednego, Mary, John the Baptist, Peter, Paul, and Stephen.

God is calling you to courage as well. There is no doubt we will face adversity and trials in our lives. Some will be light, while others may be debilitating. I am struck by a message I heard given by an African minister who said, "In America, Christians pray for all of their pain and hardships to go away. In Africa, Christians pray for strength to deal with pain and hardships." What a difference in attitude. Which is healthier? Which group chooses not to suffer? Which is more Christlike?

Pain, suffering, trials, tribulation, and testing will come our way. We have a choice how we respond.

(4) Send in a resume.

This is one of the most powerful aspects of this story, and yet it is so easy to ignore. Jim Langley was loading lettuce and cauliflower when he decided to send in an application to one of the most prestigious jobs in all of golf. He was dreadfully unqualified and had no shot at all to get the position. Yet, he still sent in his application. I wonder how many people laughed at him when he told them what he had done. As I type that sentence, I realize the answer may have been "none" if those people knew him well and knew his character. They probably thought his leap of faith and confidence was typical for Jim. However, I do wonder what the search committee at Cypress Point initially thought when they received an application from someone so unqualified. My first impression is that they were amused at the resume from the "lettuce guy." But there was something about the application that caught their attention and kept it out of the trash can where most would have thought it belonged. Was it the courage and audacity to send in such a resume that made them think twice? Did he have three great letters of reference that intrigued the committee? Why did they not immediately dispose of Jim's laughable application?

How many times have you not done something you wanted to do because you were afraid you would be rejected or, worse yet, mocked and laughed at? Have you not applied for a job, tried out for a team, sung a solo, or asked someone out on a date? What is it? What have you really wanted to do that you didn't do because of fear? Fear of rejection. Fear of failure. Fear of being laughed at.

There is a reason the Bible says "Do not fear" 365 times. Fear and doubt are crippling, and Satan uses them masterfully to keep people from achieving their dreams, goals, and God's callings.

Several years ago, I saw this anonymous quote scribbled on a small torn piece of paper tacked on an office wall:

> You can stand outside and wonder what the answer is, or go inside and find out.

There's only one way to find out the answer. It may be "no," and it will sting for a little while. But "I'm going to take a chance on you" may be waiting behind that closed door.

> Ask, and it will be given to you; seek, and you will find; knock and it will be opened to you. For everyone who asks receives, and the one who seeks finds, and to the one who knocks it will be opened.[98]

(5) Gods' timing.

Let me ask you an uneasy question that may make you roll your eyes. "Do you think God caused me to find that magazine in December of 2011?"

In 2005, a year before this article was published, I was standing in a golf shop with Jim Langley, some 1,660 miles from my home. I saw him. His figure and mannerisms made an impact on my mind, but we never said a word to each other.

In March of 2006, this article was published. I read it and thought it was inspirational and nice, set the magazine on a shelf, and eventually forgot about it.

---

[98] Matthew 7:7–8

Five-and-a-half years later, I came across this old magazine during a time of deep despair. I read the article again, and it had a completely different impact on my life in 2011. At that moment, the story pierced my burdened heart. I knew I should not throw it away with all the other magazines because I would want to read it again later. Along with some other magazines and memorabilia, I put it in a large orange Nike shoe box that I could find easily and have read it many times since. "Suffering is a choice" is a go-to phrase that I have used many times.

Is your Bible in a special orange box you can go to time and time again for inspiration? Do you let it speak to you in different ways at different parts of your life journey?

Does God really care enough about us to do something as menial as helping us find an old magazine that he knows will impact us and turn our focus back to him? Think about how insanely simple that would be for the Creator of the universe. Would he really dabble his pinky finger in something so simple just to have me find a magazine at just the right time, or was it nothing more than a mere "coincidence"?

(6) Humility.

Simply stated, many Head Golf Professionals are exceedingly arrogant, especially those at high-profile golf courses. Even though they are employees of the club, they often dictatorially lord over all who dare enter "their domain." But, as with everything, there are exceptions. There are some who are gracious, kind, and generous. Trent Rathbun at the Whisper Rock Golf Club, Bill Stines at Silverleaf Golf Club, and Jake McCullough at Odessa Country Club are three who come to mind.

Jim Langley was the Head Golf Professional at Cypress Point Golf Club, the number 1 rated golf course in the United States. If there was anyone who was in a position to be arrogant and demanding, it was Jim. And yet, he was a man consumed with humility.

As I think of Jim, my mind goes back to the words of the Apostle Paul. Paul had asked God to remove his weakness which he called his "thorn in the flesh":

But he said to me, "My grace is sufficient for you, for my power is made perfect in weakness." Therefore I will boast all the more gladly of my weaknesses, so that the power of Christ may rest upon me. For the sake of Christ, then, I am content with weaknesses, insults, hardships, persecutions, and calamities. For when I am weak, then I am strong.[99]

Think of all that had potentially been taken from him: his livelihood, his love of playing golf, his independence, and his manhood. After his accident, no one would have blamed him if he quit his job and stayed home sitting on a couch mourning and complaining the rest of his life. And yet, in his weakness, he remained steadfast and had his greatest impact.

Suffering is a choice. Joy is a choice. Humility is a choice. And trusting God to use us for good even in our weakness is a choice. Choose wisely.

A choice

---

[99] 2 Corinthians 12:9–10

(Photo by Marcia LaRosa)

On July 20, 2013, Jim Langley died peacefully at his home, surrounded by loved ones. He was just minutes away from his seventy-sixth birthday. In an article about his passing, a past quote from Jim was provided regarding his outlook on life after the automobile accident so drastically changed his life.

"It made me realize what is truly important in life. We should challenge our comfort levels, step out of ourselves for a while and recognize that there are many who need our help and our guidance. Faith and family will get us through anything."[100]

---

[100] 99. thegolfwire.com, July 29, 2013

Chapter 9

He Checked His Watch

"For the righteous man falls seven times and rises again, but the wicked stumble in times of calamity."

—Proverbs 24:16

Why do cold fronts always hit during junior high track meets?

When my kids ran track, it seemed like every meet involved an unexpected arctic blast dropping the temperature forty degrees in thirty minutes and all would be on the verge of frostbite. And, no matter how many times we reminded our kids to take extra sweats, gloves, and a jacket, they always wound up freezing with the other kids.

My track and field experience was mediocre to say the least. I was a better-than-average runner, but it was never something I truly enjoyed. My wife, on the other hand, loves all things track. In high school, she was an Oklahoma All-State distance runner, and she understands all the aspects of conditioning and technique. Based on our life experiences, she has a greater appreciation for track and field than myself.

I enjoy watching the Olympics and college track meets because these athletes are the best in the world, and I am amazed at what they can do. But junior high and high school are a different story. Unless I have a child participating, I won't go out of my way to watch these track meets.

My middle son got the running gene from his mother. Unfortunately, he ran long-distance events, which means he ran the first event, the two-mile, and the second to last event of the meet, the mile. So we would show up at 3:00 p.m. and watch the first race, then the cold front would hit around 4:45 p.m., and the last race was always around 9:30 or 10:00 p.m.

Junior high and high school track meets are not the most thrilling events; but, as an old athlete myself, I admit there was one aspect of the meets that I found intriguing: the guy finishing last in the distance events. The most talented runners look like natural athletes with long legs and lean conditioned bodies. They have the best fitting uniforms and the highly engineered shoes weighing only a few ounces. They are well coached and have every lap technically planned. As they gracefully glide around the track, they look like they were born to run.

Then, there are the "also rans." These are the boys who are required to be in track to meet academic elective guidelines. The coach knows these kids will not generate any points at the events, and worst yet, the "also rans" are keeping the coach from spending time with the "real athletes." To be painfully blunt, many coaches consider the "also rans" a nuisance. As a result, the coach will often stick these kids in the long-distance events so he can tell them at practice to stretch for a long time and then run a few miles. This way, the coach doesn't have to be distracted with them for at least forty-five minutes to an hour.

On race day, the "also rans" look different than the other runners. Instead of expensive stealth shoes, they are wearing regular sneakers or some old basketball shoes. The sound of their heavy feet hitting the track resembles a soggy wet towel being thrown on the floor compared to the soft *tap-tap-tap* of the skilled runners. Since the "also rans" get the leftover uniforms that are too big for everyone else, they are constantly having to push their tank top sleeves back up to their bony shoulders as they run.

As the runners stepped to the starting line of this two-mile run, you could immediately tell he was an "also ran." He was shorter than the other runners, and his oversized uniform and clunky black shoes made him look even skinnier than he already was. The gun sounded, and the gazelles took off and immediately started to strategize their position in the field, while he quickly assumed his place in the back. Depending on the length of the race, there is always the chance the "also rans" will get lapped. Truthfully, it is a sad scene to watch as you wonder what is going through their minds. Are they humiliated because it is painfully obvious to everyone in the stands that they are subpar athletes? Do they wonder if their parents are embarrassed that they aren't as good as the other kids? Do their parents even come and watch them race because they know their child will finish dead last, and who has time to waste? Does their coach yell at them because of their slow times, or do they even get any attention at all?

The skilled runners are graceful. They have a rare God-given gift that is pleasurable to watch. On the final lap, there were four runners in the lead group as they made the final turn. As one runner faded, the three leaders raced down the final straightaway with grit, determination, and pain on their faces. The individual muscle fibers bulged in their thighs and calves as they strained toward the finish line. Fellow students and parents in the stands screamed wildly for the runner from their school. This is the essence of competition. One runner had a last-second burst of energy as he leaned forward at the tape and he beat the other runners by just a fraction of a second. The coaches and other athletes ran onto the track and congratulated the exhausted runners while telling them to "stand up and let oxygen get to your lungs." The times were posted on the scoreboard, and the fans cheered the victors. All the while, he was still on the track. He got lapped earlier, and he was just now starting his eighth and final lap. As he reached the finish line area, he had to avoid the coaches and other runners who weren't thinking about the fact that there was still another runner on the track. He was easily going to finish three or four minutes behind the winner, but his stride had remained steady and resolute. There were other slow runners in this race, but even they were well ahead of him. It's getting late, and the event coordinators were quickly trying to get the next race set up, but they had to wait for him. They did not hide their frustration. The lighting at the stadium wasn't very efficient past the football end zones, so he was kind of in a dark place as he rounded his final turn. Then something interesting started to happen. It was hard to recognize at first, but it appeared he was picking up speed. As he entered the final straightaway, he was in his kick.

This was when the lump filled my throat. This boy was from another school and I didn't know him, but I was so proud of him. As an athlete, I know what he was experiencing. He was tired. He was likely discouraged and embarrassed. But he had staying power. My first thought was somewhere, somebody taught him the importance of finishing what you started. But I also wondered if it was simply something within his core that told him to keep going. This determination even in the face of glaring defeat is a rare commodity, especially in someone so young.

He got to the last one hundred yards, and he was in a dead sprint. He was running his race. He did not care that he was going to finish dead last. He was going to finish. I started to clap for him. He did not care that everyone was waiting on him to start the next race; he was running his race, and he was going to finish. Several more people in the stands started to clap, some out of encouragement, some out of embarrassment. The sleeve on his right shoulder had slipped down to his elbow, but his arms were pumping, and he's lifting his boney knees high as he strained toward the vacant finish line. He was determined. He was focused. As he neared the finish line, he leaned forward, and then he checked his watch. I immediately started laughing as I tapped April on the shoulder and asked, "Did you see that? He checked his watch! That's awesome!" This boy who finished dead last looked at his watch to check his time. Did he meet his goal? Was it his personal best? Was he disappointed or excited? I don't know. But I do know he finished his race. He didn't care that he was dead animal in the road last; he only cared about how he ran his race. He didn't care who the other runners were or what their times were; he cared about how he ran his race. It was awesome! He finished! I watched as he walked toward his crumpled blue gym bag lying on the grass of the football field. One teammate softly patted him on the back, but no coaches said anything to him. He simply walked over to his bag, quickly put on some sweats that were at least a size too big, slung the bag over his shoulder, and walked away.

Where does that determination come from? Where does that heart come from?

I wish I knew what happened when he got home that night. Did he excitedly tell his parents about the race, and were they thrilled with his success and did they offer encouragement? Or did he quietly tell them his time and was met with the disappointment and failure he had grown so accustomed to? Did he go to bed satisfied? Did he sleep well that night? I have no idea. I just know he gave a man, a father, in the stands an example of determination and focus; and now I am writing about it for you.

I truly love the world of sports. I was extremely fortunate to play as a youth and even play baseball at the college level. Even though you truly don't appreciate it until your playing days are over, I was able to see that sports can teach a lot of life lessons about perseverance, integrity, honor, character, endurance, mental and physical strength, and staying power. I also believe sports have the ability to inspire. And through the popularity and influence of sports, you have the ability to reach a wide variety of people.

It is interesting when I read the Bible and especially when I read the writings of Paul, I see how sports are used to touch a wide variety of people. And you might think it odd, but I believe Paul was a great fan of sports.

We tend to think of Paul as this nerdy Bible-thumping guy who was always so serious and stern all the time, but I believe if there was anyone who understood the pure joy of living a life of enthusiasm and determination, it was Paul. When you examine the ups and downs of his life, it is obvious that much of his approach to life was because he knew so intimately the benefits of discipline, determination, and focus. I picture Paul on his feet in the stands at sporting events, and he is cheering those athletes on, and he is craning his neck to see who is coming down the last straightaway to win the race. He is clapping and yelling encouragement as the runners fight for position and reach deep in their inner being for all the strength and nerve their bodies can provide. He watches and appreciates their endurance and all it takes to be victorious, and he is inspired.

When I read the writings of Paul, I see instance after instance of athletic imagery being used to make a point. And with the athletic references that occupy so much of the writings to Timothy, I am convinced that Paul and Timothy must have gone to sporting events together and shared an appreciation for the games and the athletes. I can picture them cheering in the stands; and after the events are over, I can see them at home eating dinner and talking about all the events and athletes they watched that day, just like we do.

One of the things I think is interesting about Paul is the time he spent in Corinth, not only because Corinth was a melting pot of a lot of people and cultures but because Corinth was home to the Isthmian Games, which were widely popular sporting events that took place opposite years of the Olympics. People would travel for many miles and from different countries just to watch these sporting events in Corinth. So basically, all of these people were coming to where Paul was conducting his preaching and training, and Paul was using this opportunity to share the gospel and have it spread throughout the world when those people would return to their home countries.

One of the most remarkable aspects of the Isthmian Games was that the athletes couldn't just show up and participate. The athletes had to prove they were serious athletic competitors and had to have witnesses that they had been in training for a minimum of ten months. As a result of this rule, many of these athletes would come to Corinth ten to twelve months early for their training; and then before competing, they were required to sign an oath promising they would participate with honor.

I can see Paul as he was walking around Corinth and he was watching these athletes in training and that inspired him in his future writings because he knew the use of these images would resonate with many other people. He might be walking through the city and seeing wrestlers in training, and Paul thought about that as he later wrote in Ephesians 6:12, "For we do not wrestle against flesh and blood, but against the rulers, against authorities, against the cosmic powers over this present darkness..."

Or maybe he was talking with some friends, and out of the corner of his eye he noticed some archers as they were practicing; and then he wrote about "missing the mark" and "going astray," as we see in 1 Timothy 1:6, "...from which some, having missed the mark, have turned aside to meaningless discourse,"[101] and in 2 Timothy 2:18 where it says, "...who have gone astray concerning the truth."[102]

Or maybe Paul was working to repair someone's tent, and in the distance he saw a fighter who was shadowboxing; and Paul thought about that as he wrote in 1 Corinthians 9:26, "So I do not run aimlessly; I do not box as one beating the air. But I discipline my body and keep it under control, lest after preaching to others I myself should be disqualified."

In all of these athletic images that Paul wrote about, the one he seemed to write the most about is races and how he compared life to races. We see in 1 Corinthians 9:24, "Do you not know that in a race all runners run but only one receives the prize? So run that you may obtain it." Philippians 3:14 states, "I press on toward the goal for the prize of the upward call of God in Christ Jesus." Probably his most famous reference to races is in 2 Timothy 4:7 where he said, "I have fought the good fight, I have finished the race, I have kept the faith."

After the races, I see Paul watching an awards ceremony and paying close attention to the judges. He watched closely because in the Isthmian Games, there would be a judge assigned to the event and the judge would determine whether or not the athlete competed within the rules and had competed with honor. Even if an athlete had won the event, if the judge declared they had done so dishonorably, the crown would not be given to them. So, immediately after Paul had written about fighting a good fight and finishing the race, he interjected the idea of the judge as he wrote in 2 Timothy 4:8, "Henceforth, there is laid up for me the crown of righteousness,

---

[101] 1 Timothy 1:6 (Berean Literal Bible)
[102] 2 Timothy 2:18 (Berean Literal Bible)

which the Lord, the righteous judge, will award to me on that day, and not only to me but also to all who have loved his appearing."

Paul was continually writing about competing and living with honor, endurance, and perseverance.

In all these passages about races, there is one in particular that intrigues me. It is in Galatians 5:7 and it says, "You were running a good race. Who cut in on you to keep you from obeying the truth?" When I read that, I picture Paul up in the stands, and he is watching two runners in a race and they are neck and neck fighting for the prize. One cuts in on the other and causes them to fall off their stride. Paul then used that image as a life application when writing his letter to the Galatians.

Several years ago, I came across a video on the internet. I have no idea how many times I have watched this, but it is many. Maybe you have watched it too.

The video is of the six hundred-meter run at the 2008 Big Ten Indoor Track Championships. One of the participants was a highly successful runner from the University of Minnesota named Heather Dorniden. With only two hundred meters to go, Heather had just taken the lead from a Penn State runner and was set up perfectly for the win. Unfortunately, the two runners got their feet tangled up, and Heather fell to the ground, hard. The other three runners swerved to avoid stepping on her as she lay sprawled across lane 1. Immediately she got up, but found herself already well behind the other runners. She started running and began to gain speed. She eventually passed the Penn State runner and closed the gap with the other runners from Minnesota and Indiana University. Her expressionless face offered a fierce determination as she finally reached the other runners and leaned forward at the tape, winning by 0.04 seconds.

I watched this video many times, and I wanted to know more about Heather Dorniden. So I started reading about her and watching interviews she had given. I learned several things about her. She graduated from Minnesota and ran competitively for a few more years. She is asked to speak at a lot of events, and she has a blog. I also learned that she is a devout Christian woman. In my continued search, I watched an interview where she said on the final straightaway, "I reached a gear I never knew I had." I was immediately struck by that comment, and I have thought about it in great depth. It wasn't until she was facing adversity that she accessed something inside of her that was there all the time. She always had the ability to run that blistering pace, but never knew it. When she was forced to reach to the deepest parts of her heart, nerve, and sinew, she found something that had been there all along.

I wonder how many of us have something within us that we never knew we had. How many of us have some untapped level of skill and greatness within us? How many of us have the ability to inspire?

I look at the world that God created. I see his unequaled power and majesty and his astonishing imagination. God created the mountains, the valleys, the skies and seas, and the heavens and earth. He created irrefutable laws of nature. He set in motion principles of engineering, geometry, architecture, anatomy, physiology, mathematics, and physics to levels beyond all understanding. And in that very same breath, he created mankind in his image. He created you in his image, and he said it was good.

It seems obvious; but if God loves creating and designing as much as he does, doesn't it make sense that when he created you in his image, he would instill something extraordinary in you? Doesn't it make sense that he would put something in you that would generate immense joy when it is sought and experienced to its fullness? The pity is that because of fear or apathy, so many of us live our lives without ever tapping into those God-given talents and abilities.

When that race started, Heather was just a runner. She had no idea that fifty-eight seconds into that race her life was going to change forever. As expected, she was winning. In an instant, she got tripped, she fell, and defeat was her companion. For a split second, she had a choice. It is the same choice you and I face every single day when faced with adversity.

"Well, this isn't fair. Why does this stuff always happen to me?" Get up and finish.

"But I was doing so well and now all is lost." Get up and finish.

"But you don't understand. When I fell, it was in front of a lot of people, and I was embarrassed and humiliated." Get up and finish.

"Well, I've got to get back at that person who tripped me. They have to be punished for what they did to me." No, you've got to get up and finish. Instead of seeking vengeance and anger, get up and finish.

Fifty-eight seconds into the race, Heather had a choice to make. Fifty-nine seconds into the race, she got up. At 91.72 seconds, she finished. Somewhere in life, someone taught her about character and honor and perseverance, and that was revealed in the thirty-two seconds from the time she fell to the finish line. In thirty-two seconds, she inspired.

I think about Heather in that race and about the trials and difficulties we face, not in a race around a track, but in life. How do we respond? What determines how we respond?

You were created in the image of God. That means you have something special in you. You have the ability to overcome. You are "more than conquerors."[103] You have the ability to inspire people. And you are surrounded by people who so desperately want to be inspired. They are searching for anything that can help them through the trials and temptations of their lives. They are watching the things that you do, and they are listening to the things that you say, and they so desperately want to be inspired. And you have the ability to do that. You have the ability to inspire.

You may be asking, "How? How can someone like me inspire others?"

In Hebrews, Paul wrote:

> Therefore, since we are surrounded by so great a cloud of witnesses, let us also lay aside every weight, and sin which clings so closely, and let us run with endurance the race that is set before us, looking to Jesus, the founder and perfecter of our faith, who for the joy that was set before him

---

[103] Romans 8:37

endured the cross, despising the shame, and is seated at the right hand of the throne of God.[104]

This same passage in *The Message* translation reads as follows:

> Do you see what this means—all these pioneers who blazed the way, all these veterans cheering us on? It means we better get on with it. Strip down, start running—and never quit! No extra spiritual fat, no parasitic sins. Keep your eyes on Jesus, who both began and finished this race we're in. Study how he did it. Because he never lost sight of where he was headed—that exhilarating finish in and with God—he could put up with anything along the way: Cross, shame, whatever. And now he's there, in the place of honor, right alongside God. When you find yourselves flagging in your faith, go over that story again, item by item, that long litany of hostility he plowed through. That will shoot adrenaline into your souls![105]

How do we inspire? How do we live lives that are full and consume those hidden abilities and talents that God blessed us with? Paul said we focus on Christ alone. We lay aside every weight and sin and distraction and look to Jesus.

I think of another type of race to make this point. In horse racing, you will often see blinders that are put on horses to block their peripheral view so they are not distracted by the other horses. The jockey knows it is physically impossible for the horse to run its fastest when its head is turned and focusing on other things, so he wants the horse to only see what is in front of him. Look straight ahead. Be resolute. Be focused. This is exactly what Paul was saying in Hebrews 12: Do not let anything distract you from Jesus.

---

[104] Hebrews 12:1–2 (ESV)
[105] Hebrews 12:1–4 (The Message)

Here's the difficulty though. Satan wants you distracted constantly. And he knows the best way to keep you distracted is to tie you up in comparisons. He wants you to constantly compare yourself to other people, the person running in the race next to you. Is that person wealthier than me? Are they more successful than me? More popular? More handsome or beautiful? More intelligent? Do they have a nicer house, car, boat, furniture, and clothes? Do they have better friends? Do they have a nicer and more loving family? Do they have what I don't?

Satan wants your head on a swivel, constantly looking at other things, comparing yourself to other people. And when we compare, he is okay with you looking down on people and thinking you are better than everyone else. He can work wonders with your arrogance and pride. In your comparisons, he also wants you to feel inferior and insecure. He wants you to question God and his apportionment of worldly blessings to you. Satan loves when you dwell in doubt and timidity and bitterness. He wants you to look at trials and tribulations and blame God or wonder why God is punishing you.

God calls us to a life of joy. Satan calls us to a life of distracting comparisons. I think President Theodore Roosevelt put it best when he said, "The thief of joy is comparison."

The Apostle Paul provided an amazing admission about his struggles with comparison. In the Book of Romans, Paul was talking about the Law of Moses and living and dying by the law and the idea of sin. He was about to make a reference to the Ten Commandments.[106] Just as a reminder, here is what they are:

1. I am the Lord thy God. Thou shall not have any gods before me.
2. You shall not make for yourself an idol in the form of anything.
3. You shall not misuse the name of the Lord your God.
4. Remember the Sabbath day by keeping it holy.
5. Honor your father and your mother.

---

[106] Exodus 20:1–17

6. You shall not murder.
7. You shall not commit adultery.
8. You shall not steal.
9. You shall not give false testimony against your neighbor.
10. You shall not covet your neighbor's house, wife, or property.

In chapter 7, Paul was saying, "If it wasn't for the law, if it wasn't for this list, I wouldn't have known what sin was, and I wouldn't have known the need to return to a life of Christ." So Paul was about to make a reference to the Ten Commandments and his life. Think of what he could have chosen to use as the reminder of sin in his life. He could have chosen "don't kill, don't take the Lord's name in vain, honor your father and mother, don't lie, don't steal, and so on. Do you know what Paul chose? Coveting.

> What then shall we say? That the law is sin? By no means! Yet if it had not been for the law, I would not have known sin. For I would not have known what it is to covet if the law had not said, "You shall not covet."[107]

In all of the Ten Commandments, the one Paul said he struggled with the most is coveting, which is defined as "to desire wrongfully, inordinately, or without due regard for the rights of others: to covet another's property."[108] Paul said his struggle was coveting. Paul, this enormous giant of Christianity and selflessness, said he struggled with wanting what other people had. He struggled with comparison and looking at the runners in the other lanes.

Paul openly admitted his struggle with comparison and want. With that in mind, can you imagine his joy when he told the Philippian church:

---

[107] Romans 7:7
[108] Dictionary.com

I am not saying this because I am in need, for I have learned to be content whatever the circumstances. I know what it is to be in need, and I know what it is to have plenty. I have learned the secret of being content in any and every situation, whether well fed or hungry, whether living in plenty or in want. I can do everything through him who gives me strength.[109]

Throughout his writings, Paul was very aware of the pitfalls of comparison. But it also seems like he could turn that around and use it as a tool for ministry when others were comparing themselves to him. Paul gave the impression he was telling the Christian to take advantage of other people comparing themselves to them.

The passage in Hebrews 12 says, "...since we are surrounded by so great a cloud of witnesses..." There are two possibilities here to the meaning of that phrase. First, the use of the terms "race" and "witnesses" leads one to believe Paul could be talking about people who were physically there and observing the daily activities of believers, much like spectators at a sporting event. Or, second, it is based on the fact that the Greek-word translated "witness" is the origin of the English word "martyr."[110] Therefore, the witnesses could be martyrs who had gone before and borne witness and borne testimony with their blood. "Those who thus encompass us, a countless 'host (a 'cloud' of witnesses), have had witness borne to them through their faith, and in turn stand forth as witnesses to faith bearing testimony to its power and works."[111] It is likely Paul was referring to the heroes of faith he had just mentioned in chapter 11.

Regardless of whether it is referring to actual spectators of life or previous martyrs and faith heroes who were witnessed bearing their testimony, the idea is consistent that as a Christian, you are being watched and you have the ability to have a positive influence on peo-

---

[109] Philippians 4:11–13
[110] *NIV Study Bible* notes
[111] Ellicott's Commentary for English Readers. Biblehub.com. http://biblehub.com/commentaries/hebrews/12-1.htm

ple as you live your life as a testimony to "Christ, the founder and perfecter of our faith."

Many people do not like the idea that other people are watching them as they feel pressure to not stumble and fall. They often say, "Life is hard enough without feeling like I'm letting people down all the time." Instead of that defeatist attitude, Paul seemed to be saying, "use it as an opportunity to draw other people to Christ by the way you show endurance, focus and joy." You don't do this by being a fake Christian; you do it by living the life advised in Philippians 4:4–9:

> Rejoice in the Lord always; again I say, rejoice. Let your reasonableness be known to everyone. The Lord is at hand; do not be anxious about anything, but in everything by prayer and supplication with thanksgiving let your requests be made known to God. And the peace of God, which surpasses all understanding, will guard your hearts and minds in Christ Jesus. Finally brothers, whatever is true, whatever is honorable, whatever is just, whatever is pure, whatever is lovely, whatever is commendable, if there is any excellence, if there is anything worthy of praise, think about these things. What you have learned and received and heard and seen in me—practice these things, and the God of peace will be with you."

Paul knew it is human nature for people to compare themselves to others, and he wanted you to take advantage of it. If people want to compare themselves to you, great. Be the light of Christ and shine like "a city set on a hill,"[112] and let God be glorified. Your purpose is not to draw attention to yourself, but in living a Christ-dedicated life, you have the ability to encourage and inspire other people.

---

[112] Matthew 5:14

Let me go back to a point I made earlier. You have the ability to inspire people. There are people you come in contact with every day who are in need of something. They may be struggling with their job, marital problems, their children, low self-esteem, or a myriad of other problems of life. They are discouraged. They are frustrated. They are going through life feeling unloved and all alone even in the middle of a crowd. They are bone weary. And they are longing for anyone, or anything, to come along and offer them hope. They want to be inspired and to gain strength by the examples of others.

Do you know how I know that? Two reasons: Number one, I have been there before. You know my story. I speak from experience as one who has desperately needed to be inspired by someone and find hope. The second reason is this: As I wrote these words, I checked the internet to see how many times the Heather Dorniden race has been viewed. I was amazed at how many versions of this race now exist. There are videos from different angles in the crowd. Some videos have been modified with overlaying words and accompanying music. Some have even been translated to different languages. I scrolled down the list of videos and added the number of "views" on a calculator. I quit adding when the number reached 34,984,000 and change.

Several years after that race, in an interview with Brent Yarina of the Big Ten Network, Heather was asked, "What's the best or most memorable thing someone has told you about the race?" Heather replied:

> What's probably most powerful to me is the sheer quantity and variety of people with different backgrounds who all have felt compelled to reach out to tell me how this race has affected them. This race is so easily relatable to everyone's lives. I've heard from cancer survivors, people battling addiction, struggling artists, parents, athletes and coaches of every sport, runners of every age and ability…the list could go on. I always tell people this race isn't just about never giving up, it's

about discovering what you're capable of when you are given the opportunity to rise above adversity. I would have never guessed that getting up and finishing that race would have made me a "YouTube sensation." Not every fall I've had has been quite so epic, but I learned that it's worth getting up every time.[113]

In 2008, Heather Dorniden walked to the starting line of the six hundred-meter race, just like she had done countless times before. This was supposed to be just another race. As the starting gun sounded, she had absolutely no way to know what would happen in the next 91.72 seconds. She had no idea that in just under a minute, she was going to be faced with disappointment, embarrassment, possible injury, and loss of a race she was expected to win. Just like we experience at so many times in our lives, adversity knocks at the most inopportune time. But, somewhere in the previous twenty-one years of her life, she had been taught to think right. Maybe without even knowing, she had been exposed to something or someone who inspired her and filled her mind with a realization that she could overcome, that she could "do all things…"[114]

Where does that come from? As mentioned earlier, Paul said it comes from putting aside all the sin and everything that entangles us and focusing entirely on Jesus and the cross of forgiveness and hope.

David offered his thoughts in Psalm 121 when he said, "I look up to the mountains; does my strength come from mountains? No, my strength comes from God, who made heaven, and earth, and mountains."[115]

The same God who made the heavens and earth and mountains created you. No matter your perceived position in life, God put something in you that has the ability to inspire. He gave it to Heather

---

[113] http://btn.com/2015/06/03/a-race-to-remember-i-had-no-idea-i-fell-like-that-in-inspirational-2008-run/

[114] Philippians 4:13

[115] Psalm 121:1–2 (The Message)

Dorniden, and she has inspired more than thirty-four million people with her amazing win.

As much hope and inspiration as I find in Heather's collegiate race, I may be even more thankful when I come to the realization that God gave that same ability to inspire to a young junior high boy who finished dead last in his race. On a cold and windy Thursday night, a skinny little boy wasn't trying to do anything spectacular. Even if he was embarrassed and had to do it all alone, he simply wanted to finish his race to the best of his ability. I know, because I saw him check his watch.

I don't know if that boy has inspired thirty-four million people in his life. I doubt it. But I do know he has inspired at least one, and he did it without ever knowing. And now, just like Paul, I am writing to you about a race.

I have no way to know, but I wonder…

When he finished the race and checked his watch, instead of a time, did it say, "Well done, good and faithful servant"?[116]

Inspire someone.

It does not matter how slowly you
go, as long as you do not stop.
(Confucius)

---

[116] Matthew 25:23

Chapter 10

Stoiky Muzhik

"Yo, Adrianne."

People love movies about courage and determination. We watch movies and quietly ask ourselves, "Could that be me? Could I ever have that courage?" It is our dream and, dare I say, our fantasy.

The first *Rocky* movie came out when I was eleven years old. As a young athlete, it had a great impact on me and millions of other people who dreamed of possessing the unyielding mettle of the simple southpaw. We acted out the scenes and played the *Rocky* soundtrack as we lifted weights in a friend's garage. We grew up with Rocky Balboa throughout the following sequels, which unfortunately included *Rocky V*. In the last movie titled *Rocky Balboa*, we are taken on a forty-year trip down memory lane. As an old and out-of-shape Rocky Balboa is fighting heavyweight champion Mason "The Line" Dixon, there is a quote that sums up the entire multibillion-dollar *Rocky* franchise. In the tenth and final round, Dixon has landed a vicious right hook to the head of a battered Balboa. Falling to the ground, Rocky catches himself with a stiff left arm. The scene dramatically goes slow motion as you hear a Rocky voice-over saying:

> What is it you said to the kid? It ain't about how hard you hit. It's how hard you can get hit, and keep moving forward. How much you can take, and keep moving forward. Get up.

That is every *Rocky* movie. Against all odds, bruised, battered, and beaten, you get up and keep moving forward. The dream of every man and woman dealing with difficulties in life is simple: "Get up."

Along those lines, another favorite movie quote comes from *Bridge of Spies*. Released in 2015, this movie tells the true story of a tense period during the Cold War, when a New York lawyer named James B. Donovan (played by Tom Hanks) is recruited by the CIA to negotiate the release of a downed American pilot Gary Powers and a Russian spy named Rudolf Abel (played by Mark Rylance). Powers is being held in Russia, while Abel occupies a cell in an American prison.

Even though it is not his area of law, James Donovan is assigned as legal counsel to Rudolf Abel, an assignment that is met with scorn by fellow Americans who now view him as a traitor. To the incredulity of everyone, Donovan takes the job very seriously and works to make sure Rudolf Abel is treated fairly according to the US Constitution. Even though the law is on his side, in the highly charged Cold War political atmosphere, Donovan is met with defeat after defeat, and Rudolf Abel is found guilty. The next scene is in a holding room. Abel is sitting at a desk smoking a cigarette, obviously impressed by Donovan's resilience and determination in seeking blind justice. He looks at Donovan who is standing across the room and says:

> "Standing there like that, you remind me of a man who use to come to our house when I was young. My father used to say, 'Watch this man.' So, I did. Every time he came. And never once did he do anything remarkable."
>
> A somewhat confused and insulted Donovan answers, "And I remind you of him?"
>
> With respect, Abel continues, "This one time, I was about the age of your son, our house was overrun by partisan border guards; dozens of them. My father was beaten. My mother was beaten. And this man, my father's friend, he was

beaten. And I watched this man. Every time they hit him, he stood back up again. So, they hit him harder. Still, he got back to his feet. I think because of this, they stopped the beating and let him live. 'Stoiky muzhik.' I remember them saying it, 'Stoiky muzhik.' Which sort of means, like uh, standing man. Standing man."

What a powerful image—a standing man. Bruised, battered, and beaten, right is on his side as he calmly and quietly gets back to his feet and resolutely straightens his back—standing man.

My mind runs through the Bible and considers the image of a standing man, and I often think of the Apostle Paul. Resilient. Courageous. Determined. He endured beatings, floggings, and being stranded; and with each adversity he picked himself up again. The magnitude of his ministry is heightened as I read of his missionary journeys as he withstood peril and rose to stand again. *Stoiky muzhik*. But I am wondering if I may have been overlooking one of his most important episodes involves a standing man.

Before we are introduced to Saul (Paul), Acts 7 records a passionate speech made by Stephen before the leaders of the Synagogue of the Freedmen. Stephen, a follower of Jesus, powerfully called out their sin and hypocrisy. The religious leaders were threatened by this new group of religious followers, and they became enraged and savagely stoned Stephen to death. With a very simple and straightforward description, we are introduced to Saul as Acts 8:1 states, "And Saul approved of his execution."

Saul was a person of significant power, influence, and prestige. He was popular, from a well-to-do family, and was well educated. He held a position of authority among the ruling religious leaders of the day.

After the stoning, Saul was determined to imprison followers of Jesus who he believed posed a threat to Jewish religious order and, in a roundabout way, to him. With a letter of authority in hand, Saul set out on the road to Damascus. His mission was to round up followers of Christ and have them imprisoned and, in some cases, killed.

One must wonder if Saul was proud of himself. He had authority from the religious leaders to capture these people, and if he did a good job, he would no doubt get some type of public recognition or promotion. This might even be part of a three- to five-year professional progress chart he had scribbled onto a notebook. Had the men traveling with Saul been with him before on one of these raids? Did they already have a plan in place on how they would barge into the houses or places of work to capture these people? He might tear families apart, but that was none of his concern. Saul's life, and ascension to power, was falling into place perfectly.

Acts 9 records that shortly before he reached Damascus, a bright light flashed, and a loud voice was heard as Saul fell to the ground. The *Lord* appeared and confronted Saul about his persecution. The presence of the Lord left, and Saul was left blind and must be helped up by his traveling companions.

It all happened in an instant.

Take time to fully consider what was happening to Saul as he was being helped to his feet and vulnerably led into the town. Consider how his life completely changed in an instant. He was about to lose all his political and religious influence among the Jewish people; in fact, he would become an enemy of those with whom he had worked so closely. He was about to lose all his friends. He would likely lose family relationships. He would lose his job and financial stability. He was about to lose the comforts of an established home. His lifelong belief system was shattered. In an instant, everything he had worked for his entire life was gone. Only a few seconds earlier, this proud man of stature and vision was now crawling on his hands and knees in the dirt, and he was blind.

For the next few days, the irony of God was on full display. Saul had come to Damascus to capture people who believed in a man named Jesus. This man Jesus was crucified, and his lifeless body was placed in a dark tomb where he stayed for three days. Jesus was then resurrected and brought back into the light. After his encounter with the Lord, Saul lived for three days in his dark blindness, a time in which he refused to eat or drink.[117] Saul was eventually visited by Ananias, and he was transformed into the most influential Christian of all time. He is now known as the Apostle Paul.

This is an amazing story, but let's go back again and consider the story on a deeper level.

I have no way to prove what I am going to say. It is pure speculation. I have written a lot about Paul's thorn in the flesh and his three unsuccessful requests for God to take it away. The Bible never gives an indication what his thorn is, but I personally think it is a memory. I have said my thorn in the flesh is the memory of the hurt faces of my wife and children as we left our land and dream home. That memory still haunts and discourages me. I confess every time Satan wants to make me angry and question God, he flashes that tear-filled memory into the forefront of my mind. It only takes an instant. I wonder if the thorn in Paul's flesh was his memory of standing at the edge of the crowd approving of an execution while everyone laid their cloaks at his feet.[118] Some historians pronounce the mention of cloaks being laid at Saul's feet means he was in charge of the stoning. Whether he was in charge or not, the Book of Acts records that Saul "was there, giving approval" to Stephen's savage death.[119]

When Saul was watching the stoning, he no doubt had great hatred for Stephen. However, even if you hate someone, you can't help but notice courage. Even if you detest the things someone is saying, you notice when their face takes on the appearance as an angel, as did Stephen's.[120] Saul knew Stephen was fully aware the words he was saying would lead to his death, and yet Stephen stood in front of the crowd and boldly spoke truth. *Stoiky muzhik.*

As he was being stoned, Stephen victoriously prayed, "Lord Jesus, receive my spirit."[121] I wonder how many stones it took for Stephen to fall. Did he get hit, fall down, and get back up again, only to be hit with more stones? It is impossible to be certain about much,

---

[117] Acts 9:9
[118] Acts 7:58
[119] Acts 8:1
[120] Acts 6:15
[121] Acts 7:59

but I am confident of two things: Stephen died a death of incredible courage, and Saul was watching in amusement.

Stoiky muzhik.

Paul became a man of inconceivable courage and discipline. He was a spiritual giant. But I wonder if that vision of Stephen standing in front of the Sanhedrin never left his mind, much like I wonder what Peter thought every morning when he was awakened by a rooster crowing. As Stephen's courage was being played out on the stage in front of him, coats were being piled at his feet. Sadly, the coats were being laid at Saul's feet so the "rock throwers" would have better flexibility and less encumbrance. What a thought. These men in their savage condition had to remove their coats to get a better wind up to deliver a lethal pitch. In a stoning, proper protocol is for the accusers to aim at the chest of the accused. I doubt accuracy was on their minds as they hastily laid their coats at Saul's feet and picked up their hard, jagged rocks.

Throughout Paul's numerous writings, he repeatedly mentioned courage, endurance, focus, and pressing on toward the goal.[122] He also wrote specifically of a man who is meant to stand:

> Finally, be strong in the Lord and his mighty power. Put on the full armor of God so that you can take your stand against the devil's schemes. For our struggle is not against flesh and blood, but against the rulers, against the authorities, against the powers of this dark world and against the spiritual forces of evil in the heavenly realms. Therefore put on the full armor of God, so that when the day of evil comes, you may be able *to stand* your ground, and after you have done everything, *to stand. Stand firm* them, with the belt of truth buckled around your waist, with the breastplate of righteousness in place, and with your feet fitted with the readiness that comes

---

[122] Philippians 3:14

from the gospel of peace. In addition to all this, take up the shield of faith, with which you can extinguish all the flaming arrows of the evil one. Take the helmet of salvation and the sword of the Spirit, which is the word of God. And pray in the Spirit on all occasions. With this in mind, be alert and always keep on praying for the saints.[123]

Three times, Paul said to stand, to stand, and stand firm.

Many people say Paul's inspiration for this passage came from watching armored gladiators in the arena. I choose to believe it came from a man who had no literal armor on his body as he stood firm in front of an angry mob hell-bent on killing him. A man named Stephen, who had the face of an angel. A standing man. *Stoiky muzhik.*

Paul was very well versed in dealing with pain and hardship. In 2 Corinthians 11, Paul detailed some of the struggles he endured for the cross of Christ:

Whatever anyone else dares to boast about—I am speaking as a fool—I also dare to boast about. Are they Hebrews? So am I. Are they Israelites? So am I. Are they Abraham's descendants? So am I. Are they servants of Christ? (I am out of my mind to talk like this.) I am more. I have worked much harder, been in prison more frequently, been flogged more severely, and been exposed to death again and again. Five times I received from the Jews the forty lashes minus one. Three times I was beaten with rods, once I was pelted with stones, three times I was shipwrecked, I spent a night and a day in the open sea, I have been constantly on the move. I have been in danger from rivers, in danger from bandits, in danger from

---

[123] Ephesians 6:10–18

my fellow Jews, in danger from Gentiles; in danger in the city, in danger in the country, in danger at sea; and in danger from false believers. I have labored and toiled and have often gone without sleep; I have known hunger and thirst and have often gone without food; I have been cold and naked. Besides everything else, I face daily the pressure of my concern for all the churches. Who is weak, and I do not feel weak? Who is led into sin, and I do not inwardly burn?

If I must boast, I will boast of the things that show my weakness. The God and Father of the Lord Jesus, who is to be praised forever, knows that I am not lying.[124]

All of the trials and tribulations. All of the pain and suffering. How did Paul endure it all? Where did he draw the strength to "get up"? I wonder, *Did Paul draw inspiration from the vision of Stephen, a standing man?* I wonder if Paul ever said to himself, "If Stephen could do it, so can I!"

But I also wonder if the vision of Stephen falling to the ground drove Paul mad. Did Paul ever wake up at night in a cold sweat as he dreamed of the events that day? Could his mind create the feel of a cold and jagged rock in his own hand or the feel of a robe being tossed on his feet? Were the coats warm with sweat from the Jewish leaders who had worked themselves into a frenzy?

*****

What does it take to be a standing man? I believe it takes courage to stand in front of people and not care what they think of you. C. S. Lewis once said, "Integrity is doing the right thing even when no one is watching." I believe the courage of a standing man is doing what is right when everyone *is watching*.

---

[124] 2 Corinthians 11:21–31

In Matthew 5:14–16, Jesus says, "You are the light of the world. A city on a hill cannot be hidden. Neither do people light a lamp and put it under a bowl. Instead they put it on a stand, and it gives light to everyone in the house. In the same way, let your light shine before men, that they may see your good deeds and praise your Father in heaven."

An effective light is not hidden under a bowl or tucked away in an unused room in the house. It is front and center and in a position that has the most effective impact on the most people. It does not hide in the corner or crawl on the ground and hide behind a rock. It is put on a stand, and it stands firm.

Paul no doubt gained courage from his memory of Stephen's standing front and center. I also believe Paul gained strength from Jesus as a standing man.

Did Saul of Tarsus watch Jesus being crucified? As an influential person, there is a good chance he witnessed the trial and death, but we do not know for sure. But I do know he wasn't with the disciples at the Garden of Gethsemane that night.

Can you imagine the conversation when all the apostles got together for a meal or a time in learning? Can you imagine the laughter, sadness, amazement, and questions? How many times did Paul ask the apostles to describe the events at the Garden of Gethsemane? Did Peter speak up, or did he shy away from discussing that night for obvious reasons? Did Paul listen in awe? Did guilt enter his mind as he was a willing participant? Think of all the questions Paul would ask them about that night and the following morning.

Jesus was in the Garden of Gethsemane and in anguish had asked God if the cup could be passed from him, "yet not my will but thine be done." The Garden of Gethsemane was on the Mount of Olives, and the Kidron Valley was between the garden and the city of Jerusalem. Judas, the betraying disciple, was in Jerusalem; and he began to lead a group of Roman soldiers out of Jerusalem to find Jesus. John 18:3 says, "So Judas came to the grove, guiding a detachment of soldiers and some officials from the chief priests and the Pharisees. They were carrying torches, lanterns and weapons." Bible commentaries explain that a detachment, or cohort, would likely be one-sixth of a legion. This means Judas was leading at least six hundred soldiers and other officials toward Jesus. With this large number of men, the walk from Jerusalem through the Kidron Valley up the Mount of Olives and to the Garden of Gethsemane would have taken a considerable amount of time. As it was night, these men would have had many torches creating a significant source of light. From where Jesus was standing at a higher elevation, he could have watched them the entire time as they made their way toward him.

Now, if you were watching at least six hundred hardened Roman soldiers coming for you, wouldn't you do the logical thing and run and hide? That's not what Jesus did. He stood. He stood and waited for Judas, one of his twelve disciples, one of his friends. Ironically, the Book of John records that when Jesus announced who he was, the hardened, war-trained soldiers fell to the ground in fear[125]; yet Jesus stood firm.

As he was arrested, he was taken before Annas, Caiaphas, and Pilate. He stood front and center where he was visible to everyone. He stood like a city set on a hill. *Stoiky muzhik.*

When Jesus was sent to the Roman governor, Pilate, Matthew 27:11 records, "Meanwhile Jesus stood before the governor, and the governor asked him, 'Are you the King of the Jews?' 'Yes, it is as you say,' Jesus replied." From this point on, Jesus no longer spoke or made any effort to defend himself; he simply stood. Standing in front of these most politically powerful men in the world, his self-imposed silence was a death sentence. He was not hiding, but was standing like a lamp put on a stand in the center of a room. *Stoiky muzhik.*

He was savagely flogged and forced to carry his own cross to Mount Calvary. Jesus was exhausted. He was weak from blood loss. He was likely naked, or close to it. The fact that Peter was warming himself by the fire tells us it was a cold morning, so Jesus would have been painfully cold. The cross was set on the ground, and Jesus was made to lie on the splintered wood. A large nail was driven into his right wrist and another into his left wrist. His feet were then lined up one on top of the other, and a single nail was driven through both

---

[125] John 18:6

feet. The cross was then raised and dropped with force into a hole that was just deep enough to hold the cross vertically. The force of the cross being dropped into the hole would have created terrible pain as the weight of Jesus's body would have been born on the nails in his hands and feet.

Physicians have written volumes about the effects of crucifixion and that the person usually dies from asphyxiation as their legs can no longer support their body and their chest muscles spasm and cause an inability to breathe. To be able to breathe, the person being crucified would literally have to push themselves up on the nail that was driven through their feet. Think just for a moment, to gain breath, Jesus was literally standing on a nail driven through his feet.

He could have run and hidden, but he chose to stand and wait on the rocky path in the garden. He could have called ten thousand angels to free him from the cross, but he chose to stand on a cruel and painful nail. Not hiding, he was standing front and center, like a city on a hill. In Matthew, Jesus says we stand for a reason. "In the same way, let your light shine before men, that they may see your good deeds and praise your Father in heaven." Jesus stood on a rusty nail in his feet so that we may praise his Father in heaven. *Stoiky muzhik*.

*****

Do you personally have a "standing man or woman" in your life, someone you can look to as an example of faithful godly living and strength? A person who stands for righteousness and honor in all circumstances? We need these people in our lives. We need mentors. We need to seek out people who are strong and courageous people of faith; and we need to befriend them. As the father told his son in *Bridge of Spies*, we need to watch them and learn from them. And we need to encourage them. They are usually not the type who crave attention or praise, but everyone needs encouragement, for it can be exhausting to be a standing man.

Sometimes, a standing man may need help up off the ground. I think of Paul on the road to Damascus. This once proud man was now blind and on his hands and knees on the dirt road. He must be helped up by the other people traveling with him. Then, he must be helped by Ananias before Paul could become the pillar of strength we recognize him to be.

Encouragement is crucial.

When I graduated from Lubbock Christian College in 1987, I asked the college president, Steven Lemley, for a letter of recommendation. In the letter, he wrote that I had "staying power." As I had never heard that term before, I looked it up and found that it means "the ability to maintain an activity or commitment despite fatigue or difficulty." I was student body president and played baseball for the college, but I have no idea what I did to cause him to write that phrase. It might have been nothing more than a form letter he gave to everyone, and I innocently assumed it was written specifically for me. Whatever the case, I consider that one of the greatest compliments I have ever received, and it has never left my mind.

It is amazing how compliments can cement themselves in your mind for so long. Form letter or not, those words had the desired effect on me. Ever since that letter of recommendation was written some thirty-four years ago, every time I have faced difficulties in life, I have tried to remind myself that someone thinks I have staying power; I can't give up. I must be a standing man.

Maybe you are like me, and you're facing a deep struggle that you simply don't understand. You feel like you're being stoned. One rock has written on it "Failure." Another rock says, "Loser," "Unreliable," "Stupid," "Lazy," "Arrogant," "Unlovable," "Disappointment," "Unrelatable," or "Ugly." The rocks keep coming from every direction. You may block a few, but you can't block them all, especially the ones that are thrown at your back. Eventually the pain and burden drops you to your knees. But one expression of encouragement can give you strength to stand again.

In all of our family struggles, I have always been most concerned about my children and how they would come out of all of this. Their faith in God is the most important thing in my life, and I did not ever want them to stumble because of my weakness or failings. I always wanted them to see their dad stand back up and keep moving forward. I'm not sure I always succeeded, but I tried. Fortunately, I am blessed with a wife who was constantly standing and offering a helping hand. I was able to gain strength from her godly "staying power." She is a "standing woman."

Encourage those you look up to and respect. Let them know they are not always standing alone. Ignoring potential harm from being associated with "this criminal," Jesus's mother Mary and John stood at the foot of the cross offering love and support. I have often wondered what encouragement that gave Jesus when he saw them and was able to speak with them.

*****

Are you a standing man or woman? Are you a person of courage and purpose willing to stand front and center like a city set on a hill?

> Be watchful, stand firm in the faith, act like men, be strong. Let all that you do be done in love. (1 Corinthians 16:13)
>
> Therefore my beloved brothers, be steadfast, immovable, always abounding in the work of the Lord, knowing that in the Lord your labor is not in vain. (1 Corinthians 15:58)

You are desperately needed, not as a fantasized movie character, but as a true standing man or woman. Our country desperately needs standing men. Our cities and communities need standing men. Your neighborhood needs standing men. Your church needs standing men. Your family needs standing men.

*****

I close in the Book of Luke with a scene from the temple. Jesus and the disciples had just watched the widow give her last two copper coins.[126] She humbly gave her all. The disciples began to talk about the beauty of the temple with its beautiful stones and precious metals. To the shock of those listening, Jesus then told how the beautiful temple would fall and be destroyed. Many scholars say this is referring to the end of the age of man, while others point to history and say Jesus was talking about the eventual fall of Jerusalem as these things came to pass within the forty-year span between Jesus's death and the fall in 70 AD. It is interesting that as Jesus was telling his disciples what would happen, he mentioned three times that they needed to stand firm:

> But before all this, they will lay hands on you and persecute you. They will deliver you to synagogues and prisons, and you will be brought before kings and governors, and all on account of my name. This will result in your being witnesses to them. But make up your mind not to worry beforehand how you will defend yourselves. For I will give you words and wisdom that none of your adversaries will be able to resist or contradict. You will be betrayed by parents, brothers, relatives and friends, and they will put some of you to death. All men will hate you because of me. But not a hair of your head will perish. By *standing firm*, you will gain life.[127]
>
> There will be signs in the sun, moon and stars. On the earth, nations will be in anguish and perplexity at the roaring and tossing of the sea. Men will faint from terror, apprehensive of what is coming on the world, for the heavenly bodies will be shaken. At that time they will see the Son of Man coming in a cloud with power and great glory. When these things begin to take

---

[126] Luke 21:1–4
[127] Luke 21:12–19

place, *stand up* and lift up your heads, because your redemption is coming near.[128]

Be careful, or your hearts will be weighed down with dissipation, drunkenness and the anxieties of life, and that day will close on you unexpectedly like a trap. For it will come upon all those who live on the face of the whole earth. Be always on the watch, and pray that you may be able to escape all that is about to happen, and that you may be able to *stand before the Son of Man.*[129]

Contentment is a journey. But many times we do not know what, or where, the destination is. It appears our ultimate destination is before the Son of Man. Sometimes, he calls us out to stand before him in a storm-filled sea. He may call us to stand with him and watch a widow give her all. He may call us to stand before our family and love them with the same love he has for his church. He may call us and ask us to stand with him as he touches the disfigured and unclean leper or heals the blind man. He may call us to stand with him as he speaks the truth to angry religious leaders or to walk through the crowd who is wanting to throw him off a cliff. He may call us to stand at a fire warming our hands and speak of our love for him when a servant girl asks if we know that man. He may call us to stand at the foot of the cross in full view of a crowd who has just nailed him to a cross.

Have I not commanded you? Be strong and courageous.
Do not be terrified; do not be discouraged, for the
Lord your God will be with you wherever you go.
(Joshua 1:9)

Stoiky muzhik

---

[128] Luke 21:25–28
[129] Luke 21:34–36

Marjorie and Walton Gooch

This is one of my favorite pictures of all time. This is my mother and grandfather. When I think of a standing man, I think of this picture—a godly man who is strong and resolute, a man who protects and cares.

Stoiky Muzhik

Be sure you put your feet in the right place, then stand firm.
(Abraham Lincoln)

Chapter 11

Answered Prayer

I asked God for strength, that I might achieve.
I was made weak, that I might learn humbly to obey.

I asked for health, that I might do greater things.
I was given infirmity, that I might do better things.

I asked for riches, that I might be happy.
I was given poverty, that I might be wise.

I asked for power, that I might have the praise of men.
I was given weakness, that I might feel the need of God.

I asked for all things, that I might enjoy life.
I was given life, that I might enjoy all things.

I got nothing that I asked for but got everything I had hoped for.
Almost despite myself, my unspoken prayers were answered.

I am, among all people, most richly blessed.

This prayer was found on a Confederate soldier's body
during the Civil War.

Chapter 12

I Don't Want to Go There

Why do we do this?

The great theologian John Pickens recently asked this question, "Have you ever gone somewhere you didn't want to go?" I can obviously think of many times as a child when my parents took me to events and places I did not want to go—adult things that are boring to kids: museums, musicals, restaurants where a tie is required, and Olan Mills Photography for the family portrait. I would also include family reunions where Great Aunt Kay, the seventy-seven-year old belly dancer, gave you a hand-sewn silk pillow that reeked of chain-smoked Marlboros. I could go on, but you get the point—places we don't want to go.

As an adult, have you ever gone somewhere you didn't want to go? Have you ever had to go to someone's house and talk about something bad your kids and their kids have done, and even though you think the parents will be highly offended, you say it is best the kids don't spend time together for a while? Have you been to the corporate function feeling totally out of place because other team members want to go to places that are against your moral judgement? Have you had to visit friends and family in hospitals and nursing homes where the smells are odd and you feel uncomfortable, the obligations to loved ones that create unease? Have you ever reluctantly gone to a part of town where you felt unsafe?

These are physical places that you simply do not want to go. You feel unease, awkward, tempted, bored, and unsafe.

John 4 tells an interesting story of a place Jews didn't want to go. The chapter starts in Judea as the Pharisees had been keeping a close eye on Jesus and noticed he was baptizing many. Even though it was the disciples who were actually doing the baptizing, there was fear rising among the Pharisees about the power and influence Jesus was harnessing. These supposed men of God could not have someone like Jesus minimizing their control over the people, and they would go to great lengths to maintain power. Jesus, aware of the potential trouble with the Pharisees, decided to travel from Judea back to Galilee, the place where he spent the majority of his ministerial life. However, in between Galilee and Jerusalem was Samaria, a land despised by the Jews. It was a mutual loathing; the Jews hated the Samaritan Gentiles and the Samaritans hated the Jews. When required to travel from Judea to Galilee, rather than walking the straight route through Samaria, the Jewish people would typically walk east, cross the Jordan River, walk north, cross the Jordan River again, and walk west to Galilee. The trip was considerably longer, but it avoided the land of wretched Samaritans.

As I have mentioned before, there is great revelation hidden in small phrases in the Bible. Another example arises in John 4:4 where it reads, "Now he had to go through Samaria." At first glance, one would easily say that is simply an untrue statement; it is a lie. Jesus did not "have to" go through Samaria. Like all the other Jews, he could walk the long way around. So why does the text say, "…he had to go through Samaria"?

Don't you know the disciples were asking the same thing? How many times do you think they asked Jesus why they were doing something as nonsensical as walking through the despised land? How many times did they ask why he was doing specific things that seemed irrational, breaking century-old customs, turning over tables of the money changers, offending people of power and influence, eating meals with tax collectors and prostitutes, touching the unclean, siding with an adulterer, giving audience to women, letting children sit in his lap, saying you must eat his flesh, and so on?

We see the frustration of the disciples in John 11 where Lazarus had died and Jesus said he wanted to go to Judea. The disciples told him this made no sense and warned him "the Jews were just now seeking to stone him."[130] Unwavering, Jesus started to Judea. "So Thomas, called the Twin, said to his fellow disciples, 'Let us go that we may die with him.'"[131] What an odd statement. Thomas was basically saying, "Oh well, if he's going to die, we might as well die with him." Why would Thomas say that?

How many times do you think the disciples shook their heads and whispered to each other, "Man, he is going to get us in so much trouble"?

How many times do you think the disciples asked themselves, "Why are we doing this? Why do we follow this man?"

Have you ever asked that question? Why do I follow this man Jesus? Sometimes life would seem so much easier if I lived life out from under his influence. It would be easier if I wasn't letting him lead me to places I don't want to go.

What does John 4:4 really mean? Why did he have to go through Samaria? Think about all that happened in this short story.

Jesus and the disciples traveled into Samaria, a place they did not want to go. They got to a well, and Jesus asked the disciples to do the unthinkable: go into a Samaritan town called Sychar and do business with a shopkeeper for food and supplies. The disciples were now having to go even further into the place they did not want to go, and they were giving their money to a despicable Samaritan shopkeeper.

While the disciples were gone, a Samaritan woman came to the well. It was a place she did not want to go. It was normal for women of the town to go to the well in the morning when the temperature was cool. However, the well would be busy that time of day, and this woman was obviously not welcome or comfortable with the other women. It was likely her background and relationships with her five husbands that made her an outcast. Like most, she probably longed for friendships and to share the joys of communal life. But she was lost and lonely, and she went to the well during the heat of the day. It was physically uncomfortable, but it was a time when she could be

---

[130] John 11:8
[131] John 11:16

alone—until one day. On this day, there was a strange Jewish man sitting on the edge of the well looking at the cool water below. And this man, a Jew, had the unmitigated gall to ask her for a drink of water from the well. Consider her shock and astonishment in this unusual man.

We know the rest of the beautiful story as Jesus talked to her about living water and how one day the Jew and Gentile would worship together. She said she had heard of the Messiah, and Jesus revealed himself to her.

Just then, the disciples came back. Can't you picture them a couple hundred yards from the well and they thought they saw Jesus talking to someone, a woman? Which disciple was the first to grumble, "Aw man, what's he doing now? Is he talking to a Samaritan woman? He's gonna get us in so much trouble!" But notice verse 27 says, "They marveled that he was talking with a woman, but no one said, 'What do you seek?' or, 'Why are you talking to her?'" Were they too afraid to ask him to his face what they asked each other at a distance? The disciples had no idea what had happened while they were gone. All they knew was, as they walked up, she left her jar by the edge of the well and ran off into town. So they did what any man would do; they started talking to Jesus about food. Soon, she returned with other people from the town, and they wanted to learn more about Jesus. The Samaritan Gentiles from town asked Jesus and his disciples to stay two days, which they did.

> Many Samaritans from that town believed in him because of the woman's testimony, "He told me all that I ever did." So when the Samaritans came to him, they asked him to stay with them, and he stayed there two days. And many believed because of his word. They said to the woman, "It is no longer because of what you said that we believe, for we have heard for ourselves, and know that he is indeed the Savior of the world."[132]

---

[132] John 4:39–42

The despised land of Samaria—instead of avoiding it like all Jews did, they walked through it. Instead of walking as quickly as possible, Jesus lingered at a well. Instead of leaving quickly after his drink, they all stayed two extra days. Can you imagine what the disciples were thinking? Were they seeing the beauty and magnitude of what was happening, or were their prejudices blinding their eyes? Was this why Jesus sent them into town to buy supplies? Did Jesus send them into a place they did not want to go because he knew they would just be in the way at the well when the woman came? Did Jesus know he would have to waste precious time arguing with them about talking to a Samaritan woman versus the quality time he could spend with her in private?

I wonder, *Has God ever moved me out of the way so that he could work with someone? Have I ever been a hindrance on someone's spiritual growth and God gently moves me aside for a while or moves me out of someone's life completely?*

And what about the woman? Embarrassed. Lonely. Yet, receptive. This woman ran to town and led people back to the well to see and hear Jesus, and many believed and were saved. Of all the people in the world, this lowly Samaritan woman who walked alone out to a well in the heat of the day hoping to avoid people became the first recorded evangelist for Jesus Christ. As a result, two thousand years later, we are telling the story of going to places we don't want to go and seeing the fruit that is produced.

John Pickens tells of the story of his beautiful daughter, Montana, and her twenty-month battle with cancer. John was a preacher and teacher at the onset of her illness, and he had to retire so he and his wife could take turns during the day and night to care for her. As her health declined, Montana was moved from Oklahoma to a hospital in Atlanta where she spent the last two months of her life.

With eloquence and grace, John tells of being taken to a place where he did not want to go. That place was not a physical place like a hospital in Atlanta. It was the emotional and soul-stirring place of dealing with the loss of a child, a place of unequaled pain and sorrow, the place of heartbreaking "Why?"

John and Lisa Pickens are confident Montana is in the presence of God Almighty; she is experiencing the ultimate reward of pure joy. That belief allows John to say, "God will never take me to a place I don't need to go. When I go through a tough time, how am I on the other side of it? Have I improved as a person?" He speaks of the lessons learned, the grace and mercy he feels, knowing the importance of each life and the impact one solitary life can have on many. During Montana's sickness, John was wandering through Samaria. It was a place he did not want to go. But he came out on the other side a stronger and better man.

The painful loss of my mother and mother-in-law. The loss of our dream house and land. The deep financial worries and hardships we endured as a family. My deep feelings of failure as a dad and husband. The loss of dear friends as we were forced to move to a different city. My emergency surgery in a town away from family and friends. Car troubles. Lack of food. Trials and tribulations. Pain and sorrow. All places I did not want to go. But I ask, "How am I on the other side of it?"

I have spent much time trying to understand James 1:2–18. How do I find joy in trials and tribulations? How do I find joy when led into places I do not want to go? What an irrational thought. But, as I consider this, I wonder if my attitude about trials would be different if I looked at every one of them with the mind-set that "God will never take me to a place I do not need to go." What would the outcome be if I stared straight into the face of each trial and said, "I may not like it here, but God is intentionally leading me to this place because I will be a better person on the other side of it. Trust. Obey. Endure. Grow. Be joyful in Christ alone."

The Message translates James 1:2–4 as follows:

> Consider it a sheer gift, friends, when tests and challenges come at you from all sides. You know that under pressure, your faith-life is forced into the open and shows its true colors. So don't try to get out of anything prematurely. Let it do its work so you become mature and well-developed, not deficient in any way.

What can God do with me in the places I don't want to go? The lesson from the well is Jesus picked some low-hanging fruit. A woman presented an opportunity for conversation, and Jesus took it.

It is the same with us. We are in our own "Samaria," although yours may be called Texas, Oregon, Michigan, or New York. What are we doing in our Samaria? Are we picking the low-hanging fruit so evident around us, or do we instead seek and walk into places that are comfortable and require no work? Why do we seem to concentrate so much on foreign mission fields and leave the ripe fields directly around us unpicked? Is it because the foreign mission field is one we can dedicate one or two weeks to and then return to our home, whereas the mission field around our home is one we can't easily leave and it begs consistency?

Why does John 4:4 say, "Jesus had to go there"? It had nothing to do with it being a shorter walk. It was because Jesus knew there was an opportunity that could change not just one life, but potentially many others. It was his mission. It was his purpose for being on earth. To fulfill his purpose, "he had to go." The field was ripe for harvest, and he must talk to a lonely woman coming to a well in the heat of the day.

What is your purpose? What is my purpose?

Did God take me on this journey to improve me? I admit I have not enjoyed this journey. It has been hard and painful. But I wonder, *All this time, was God taking me where I needed to go and maybe I am just now removing the scales from my eyes and seeing with clearer vision? Did he take me here to learn about the destructive nature of pride and the beauty and joy of humility? Was it to learn to trust and obey? Was it to learn to love others more openly? Did he lead me here to learn to be a better receiver of gifts and blessings? Did he lead me here because he loves me?*

It has taken me a long time to understand that God has led me into this storm because he loves me and knows I will be better because of it. My question is now, "What kind of man will I be on the other side?"

Where is God taking you? Are you being led into an uncomfortable land, where you may experience hardships and pain? What is it you may be being asked to learn? Is there an area of your life that you see an opportunity to grow and develop?

The storm is hard. I keep telling God the ship is difficult to man by myself when the winds and waves are tossing me around like a rag doll. I cry out to Jesus and wonder why he doesn't care that I perish. He gently reminds me that the wind and waves still know his name.

I often think of the story of Peter walking on water. Matthew tells of Peter asking to come out to Jesus, and as he was walking on the water, he became afraid of the wind and waves. Jesus saved Peter, and Matthew 14:32–33 says, "And when they got into the boat, the wind ceased. And those in the boat worshiped him, saying 'Truly you are the Son of God.'"

There are two things that strike me here. First, why didn't Jesus calm the wind and waves before he asked Peter to join him? Walking on calm water would have still been an amazing miracle, but why did he call Peter out into a storm? Second, was this encounter for the benefit of Peter or the others in the boat, the eleven spectators?

Are you being led into a storm for your benefit or the benefit of others around you? Has God blessed you with the honor of experiencing hardships so that others can see how you respond and they will then be drawn to the glory of God? Is your spouse benefitting from the way you are responding? Are your children, or other family members, benefitting from your response to the storm? I can think of no greater gift to give your children than for them to see you in full obedience and trust in God in the midst of a storm. What a blessing.

> Blessed is the man who remains steadfast under trial, for when he has stood the test he will receive the crown of life, which God has promised to those who love him. (James 2:12)

*****

Praise God for the storm.
Keep rowing.
Be a better person when you get to the other side.

Chapter 13

A Holy Task

Written by Margie Stephenson

Oh, if we had the gift to see
What the molding of a child will really be.

The routine tasks we daily work through,
We wonder just what good they do.

This child, so little, requires so much;
My world is different; I feel so out of touch.

The books make it sound like I should be so complete,
Baby all happy and house so neat.

I'm not at all certain how to handle each day;
Make me wise and content as I go along the way.

Oh, God, please give us the gift to see
Just what the molding of a child is to be.

The things they see and feel in us
Will teach them who and what to trust.

Please give me a glimpse of how important my task
So I will not sink under this routine mask.

Give me wisdom and stamina, dear Lord
To help my family walk with you in one accord.

Keep my spirits lifted I ask
Knowing I've been chosen for a holy task.

Chapter 14

Time and Proximity

What is a wasted life?

One of my biggest fears had been living a wasted life, a life of no consequence or meaning. I did not want to be someone who just lives and dies and leaves no mark of existence—nothing conquered, nothing gained, nothing of value or meaning left behind.

For twenty-eight years, my occupation and identity was "golf course architect." I traveled the world designing and building golf courses, resorts, and residential developments. Talk to most designers or architects, and you will find a common goal of leaving behind some great structure that will be admired—the Eiffel Tower designed by Gustave Eiffel, New York's Central Park designed by Frederick Law Olmsted, Augusta National Golf Club designed by Bobby Jones. It is leaving something behind that says, "I lived a life that generated something of value and worth." I lived.

Pride

I admit I fell deep into that trap—pride. I wanted to create golf courses that would live long past my time on earth. It was common for me to be wearing a hat or shirt from a golf course I designed and have someone come up to me in the airport and say, "What a great course...have you played there?" And I could act all humble and say, "Well, actually, I designed it..." Then I could revel in their praise. I dreamed of my children taking their children and grandchildren to a golf course I designed and proudly telling them, "Pops built this." I wanted my children to bring their children to our dream house and forty-acre ranch north of Dallas and almost reverently tell them, "Pops built this." Ego. Self. Pride.

When the economy crashed in 2008, the unraveling began. Design jobs were lost. All income was gone in six weeks. April's mother (Nana) struggled with cancer and passed away in 2010. Her passing left a deep hole in the family soul. We then thought April had cancer in 2011. We sold off part of the ranch and lived off that money for a while. Then, we had to leave for good in 2011. At Thanksgiving 2011, April and I had to tell our kids we were about to be homeless and, in ten days, we were going to be moving to Lubbock. We were leaving relationships, friends, church, and school—everything the kids knew and loved. Health issues arose. Debilitating stress was taking over my life. Anxiety. Weight gain. Crushing financial hardships. Failure. Embarrassment. Spiritual doubt. Fatigue. A wall of bricks crashing down. I was helpless to stop any of it. If I was not in full clinical depression, I had at least one foot in the pool. In one of my darkest hours, I dejectedly told April, "I feel like I have lived a totally wasted life." Her immediate anger was startling as it was so uncommon. April is normally a very kind, quiet, and deeply respectful person; but my comment set her off. "How can you say that? I am deeply offended by that!" She forcefully continued, "Is our marriage a waste? Are our kids a waste?" She kept going, but I admit I don't remember much of what she said after that initial volley as I was immediately knocked back on my heels realizing she was right. My deeply bruised pride had caused me to say something foolish, and to this day, I wish I could take back.

What is a wasted life?

What is a life of value?

I was living these questions and struggling to find an answer. Interestingly, my answer may have been found in a box in the garage containing old worn-out gloves.

Worn-Out Gloves

Worn-out gloves mean something to me. Worn-out gloves give testimony to hard work and perseverance. I have always wanted to outwork the person next to me, and worn-out gloves mean I was willing to go the extra mile and work a little harder. A small hole would start from wear and tear, and you simply put duct tape on it and keep going. Don't let anything stop you.

Worn-out gloves. Callouses. Strong hands.

As strange as it sounds, I have always been fascinated by a handshake. I believe you can tell a lot by someone's hands. When shaking hands, you sense someone's physical strength. A strong calloused hand gives testimony to hard work, even though no words are spoken. A firm handshake can speak to self-confidence or respectful manners. Dark and tanned hands advertise work in the sun, while pale hands testify to being indoors.

My mother's father was "Pappaw," and I distinctly remember his hands. Pappaw passed away suddenly from a heart attack while I was in my twenties. At his funeral, I remember standing at his coffin and being shocked as I looked at his hands. Pappaw was a man's man—strong, athletic, a man who worked with his hands. When I was around thirteen years of age, I remember standing in the kitchen, and Pappaw walked by and slapped me on the back. *Boom.* It was not out of anger, but simply the way men say "hello." While his hand was powerful, and just a little painful on my back, I remember thinking at that moment, *He must think I'm strong enough to take that blow.* It meant a lot to me. In life, his hands were always strong and powerful. Now, in death, his hands looked thin and frail. His ring was even loose on his finger. I distinctly remember thinking, *That's not Pappaw.* That man was not Walton Gooch.

In memory of Pappaw, my oldest son's middle name is Walton. When my son was getting married, he wanted some wedding pictures wearing some of Pappaw's old fedoras we had stored in a box in the closet. I opened a box and began to raise a hat to my head. As the hat got close to my face, I immediately smelled Pappaw.

Pappaw had a very distinct smell. It wasn't a stink by any stretch. His smell was a combination of aftershave lotion, saw dust, pine trees, and time. I smelled the hat and was immediately taken back to my childhood and visits to his small house in Muskogee, Oklahoma, sitting in the green recliner listening to the police scanner. Great memories.

I think of that hat and wonder, *Do you think it's odd to say you know someone by their smell?* One's first reaction may be "That's gross." But do you joyfully know someone by their smell?

Does the smell of fresh bread take you back to wearing a large apron and standing on a chair in the kitchen to help your mom as she made her famous homemade bread?

Does the smell of a mechanics garage take you back to helping your dad change the oil in the car?

Does the smell of hay take you back to your grandpa's farm and feeding cows?

Can smell trigger memories of people?

In reading the Book of Genesis, I'm struck by a simple line in the very familiar story of Jacob stealing the blessing that belonged to Esau. In chapter 27, we read that Jacob and Esau's father, Isaac, was basically blind. Isaac intended to meet with Esau, but Rebecca (Isaac's wife) and Jacob tricked him into believing Jacob was actually Esau. One of the ways intended to trick Isaac was having Jacob wear Esau's clothes. In verse 27, Jacob went into Isaac's room; and the text says, "…when Isaac caught the smell of his clothes, he blessed him and said, 'Ah, the smell of my son is like the smell of the field that the Lord has blessed.'"

Isaac recognized the smell of Esau's clothes. Many commentaries say this was not an odorous smell but more of an aromatic smell of flowers, grasses, and bushes of the field. I'm not sure how they know that, and I don't want to concentrate on what type of smell it was but simply that Isaac knew the smell of his son's clothes.

How can that be?

What does that tell you?

When I smelled Pappaw's fedora hats, my mind was instantly transported to the old green cloth recliner listening to the police scanner hoping Uncle Allen would drive by and say "Hey, Gooch" from his police car. When he would, we would run out in the front yard and hope to get a glimpse of his red taillights down the street. The smell of the hats took me back to the front seat of the tan four-door Buick as we drove over the speed limit on backroads to the hardware store. The smell was sitting on the bench under the pine trees at the ice-cream shop across the street from their house. The smell was sitting in the church pew next to Pappaw and listening to him trying to mumble sing. He was a bad singer.

Time and Proximity

I recognized his smell, even after he had been gone for more than twenty years. What does that mean to you? To me, it means two things: time and proximity. Time. The only way I knew the smell of Pappaw was because he spent time with me. He gave me the most valuable thing he could give: his time. He gave me part of his life.

Proximity. The common denominator of every one of those memories was that I was sitting next to him—the recliner, front seat of the car, bench under the tree, and the pew at church. I was literally next to him.

Time and proximity.

The only way Isaac knew the smell of Esau was by spending time with him and being close to him.

I read that and ask, "Did they spend time together in the tent talking and laughing?"

"Did Isaac love hearing Esau's stories of stalking game on the hunt?"

"Did they sit next to each other during meals?"

"Did they go on walks together in the fields with Esau having to hold up an aged Isaac as he couldn't see or traverse the path very well?"

"On a cool chilly night, did they sit together by the fire and discuss the goodness of God as they stared at the stars?"

How did Isaac know the smell of Esau?

This is such a sad part of the Bible. It is a story of family deception, greed, and theft. It is dishonesty in a marriage. It is a son not honoring his father. And yet, tucked in between all the ugliness is this beautiful story of relationship revealed simply by recognizing the smell of someone.

Do you know the smell of your children because you frequently give them a hug?

Do you know the smell of your spouse because you've spent time lying next to them in bed just talking about the day?

Do you know the smell of your parents or friends from the time you've sat next to them on the couch?

Time and proximity.

Why do I tell you this? While working as a golf course architect, I spent many days and nights on the road. I was away from the family—alone. One particular trip to Thailand was very tiring, tough, and literally dangerous. I had been gone more than a week, and I got home in the middle of the night. My boys were very young, and I went to their shared bedroom. The room was dark except for a small nightlight. For a long time, I sat against the wall and watched them sleep. I looked at their quiet faces and wondered what their eyes would see as they grew older. I hoped innumerable scenes of beauty and grace would outweigh the ugliness and horror that can easily overwhelm. I watched their chests rise and fall with each breath, and I wondered what words they would say as they grew older. I prayed their words would be kind, encouraging, and honorable rather than divisive and hurtful. I also looked intently at their hands. Their fingers were so small. I looked at their hands and wondered what they would do with them as they grew older. Would they hold a baseball bat? Would they throw a football with a tight spiral? Would they play the keys of the piano or pluck the strings of a guitar? Would those hands hold the hand of a woman they would love and marry and their ring finger display the symbol of that love? Would those hands one day hold a child of their own? I also prayed those hands be strong and calloused from hard work. I prayed their hands would be used for good and not for evil.

Many years passed from that quiet night. Those small boys are now strong young men, and their younger sister is a beautiful young woman.

After losing the ranch and moving from the Dallas area, I was struggling with the feeling of living a wasted life. Satan had done a masterful job of dulling my eyes to God's numerous blessings, and I was only recognizing misery. During one of our moves, I was cleaning the garage and moving boxes containing dusty sports gears, old basketball shoes and cleats, batting helmets, shin guards and chest protectors, footballs that had lost some air, various baseball and softball gloves the kids had used throughout the years, numerous old and cracked batting gloves, and sticky gray football receiver and quarterback gloves. I mentioned earlier that I prided myself on having worn-out gloves. To me, a worn-out glove is a symbol of hard work, sweat, and blood. The worn-out gloves also represent time. It takes time to wear out gloves.

I sat in the garage looking at the old gloves in the boxes. Each one brought back memories. There were countless hours playing catch with a baseball in the front yard or working on pitching motions in the high school bullpen or hitting thousands of fungo to the kids at shortstop and centerfield. And, of course, there was batting practice. How many hundreds of thousands of pitches were thrown to three baseball players and a softball player, and their teams, over twenty-plus years?

I looked at the worn-out gloves and thought about the boys' hands and my prayer that night long ago when they were so small. These worn-out gloves were the work of those hands.

The boxes in the garage also contained pictures. Some were of construction of our house and the kids helping dig trenches for water and irrigation lines. There were pictures of the kids helping set green metal T-posts and running barbed wire for pasture fences. In these pictures, the kids were wearing gloves that were dirty and sweaty.

The worn-out gloves and photographs were memories—memories involving time and proximity.

The bank may take homes and land, but their reach does not include memories. Building the house and pool. Bribing the kids with

$0.75 canned soft drinks from Home Depot to install large amounts of sod in the front yard. Feeding the longhorns. Firework parties and cookouts on the fourth of July with friends and family. Trying to figure out what to do with years' worth of plastic sports trophies and deciding to line them up in the pasture and letting the kids joyfully blow them away with a twelve-gauge shotgun. Memories. Time and proximity.

Memories. Laughter. Pain. Joy. Tears. Happiness. Anxiety and depression. Fear. Failure. Doubt. Hope. Commitment. Love. Contentment.

Without realizing, contentment had crept in.

Contentment. Isn't that an interesting word? We strive our entire lives to reach bigger and better things. We set lofty goals and often find the goal posts have moved somewhere along the way. We always seem to be chasing. Satan is a master of marketing and making us feel like we need more and we deserve more. We, I, are constantly trying to keep up with what others have and struggle with feelings of failure and not measuring up. It is so hard to ever find contentment.

I tearfully looked at, and held, the worn-out gloves and felt contentment and joy because each stain, hole, and rip reveals a memory and represents time and proximity with my children—sharing life with those you love. Value.

While the joy in seeing these gloves was great, my joy was greater when two other items were found in the boxes…two Bibles.

*The first Bible…*Brooks has had the "brown Bible" for quite some time. It was his favorite, but it went missing for several years even though Brooks would often look for it. This particular day, we were cleaning boxes out of the garage and throwing stuff away. We had moved a couple of times and figured that since these boxes had never been opened, we must not need any of this stuff as it must not be too important. Going through one of the boxes, I came across the brown Bible. Along with other books, it had been put in this box, and I'm sure Brooks just forgot which box it was in. Our move from Celina was such an emotional time; it's a wonder we could find anything in any of the boxes we packed.

We happily texted Brooks to let him know that "ole' brown" was found, and he asked us to bring it to him at college on our next visit. That simple request led me down a path of thought and reflection that I would like to share.

The Apostle Paul has always been a favorite of mine. I study his writings and feel like there is something new to learn with each reading. Maybe God chooses different times to enlighten our readings. I am intrigued by so many things Paul said, but one that creates great focus is his statement in Philippians 4:11 where he said, "I am not saying this because I am in need, for I have learned to be content whatever the circumstances."

Dictionary.com defines contentment as "The state of being contented; satisfaction; ease of mind."

Paul famously said, "I have learned to be content whatever the circumstances." How can that be? Paul had lived his early life as a person of privilege and learning. He was from a wealthy family and had status among his peers. He was used to nice things and was likely never in want. Power, privilege, prestige, purpose...all lost as he crawled blind on his hands and knees in the rocks and dirt on the road to Damascus. For three days he was blind. Try to truly consider the magnitude of change in his life. For three days his world was dark, almost as if he was in a cave or tomb. Everything he was brought up to believe was turned upside down. He was so sure, confident, and focused on "saving God" from these blasphemous people claiming to follow this man named Jesus. Blind. He dedicated his life to Christ the Lord, and his life of adversity began. Remember what Louis L'Amour said, "There will come a time in your life when you think everything is finished. Yet that will be the beginning." This was the beginning for Paul.

He traded power and prestige for hardship. He wrote:

> I have worked much harder, been in prison more frequently, been flogged more severely, and been exposed to death again and again. Five times I received from the Jews forty lashes minus one. Three times I was beaten with rods, once I was pelted with stones, three times I was shipwrecked, I spent a night and a day in the open sea. I have been constantly on the move. I have been in dan-

ger from bandits, in danger from my fellow Jews, in danger from Gentiles; in danger in the city, in danger in the country; in danger at sea; and in danger from false believers. I have labored and toiled and have gone without sleep; I have known hunger and thirst and have gone without food; I have been cold and naked. Besides everything else, I face daily the pressure of my concern for all the churches.[133]

And yet, at the end of all of this, he spoke of contentment. Of what was the contentment born? What was Paul's secret to contentment and satisfaction? There is an overabundance of verses giving rise to Paul's deep faith and love. But, as I consider the idea of "time and proximity," I am drawn to two particular verses:

1. *1 Thessalonians 5:17* simply says, "pray continually."

Obviously, Paul was not talking about spending all day with your eyes closed and head bowed in spiritual monologue. Paul was encouraging a mind-set of being in continual presence with God; sharing in his glory and power; living each moment as an integral, active, and supporting part of his creation; and being a host of the Holy Spirit—constant communion of the mind.

2. *2 Timothy 4:13* says, "When you come, bring the cloak that I left with Carpus at Troas, and my scrolls, especially the parchments."

This is such an obscure verse, but packed with revelation. Leading up to this verse, we learn about Paul's condition and state of mind. 2 Timothy 2:9 tells us he was in chains "like a criminal." Then, in 2 Timothy 4:6–8, Paul said he knew he was at the end of his life by declaring, "I have fought the good fight."

---

[133] 2 Corinthians 11:23–28

In chains, Paul was being held unjustly in a foul-smelling, disgusting prison. He knew he was about to be executed, but he still made a request of Timothy. "When you come, bring the cloak that I left with Carpus in Troas, and my scrolls, especially the parchments."

Was he requesting the cloak because he was cold? Did he need it to roll up and use it as a pillow on the hard rock floor of the prison? Was he going to give it to another prisoner who had no clothes? We don't know.

He also asked for his scrolls. Were the scrolls copies of the Old Testament scriptures? Did Paul want to read the writings of David in Psalm 23 as he said "Even though I walk through the valley of the shadow of death, I will fear no evil, for you are with me; your rod and your staff, they comfort me" or maybe Psalm 57 where David wrote, "Have mercy on me, O God, have mercy on me, for in you my soul takes refuge. I will take refuge in the shadow of your wings until the disaster has passed"?

Were his parchments other letters he was writing to friends and churches he had established? Were these letters of encouragement, love, and training? Were these letters ever finished? Were these letters found and known to us today, or were they lost to eternity in some trash bin after Paul's death?

While we do not know what specific scripture Paul had requested, we do know he desired to be in God's Word, and I must wonder, *Was this the key to Paul's contentment? Was it all based on time and proximity with God?*

Time and proximity.

There is another lesson that tugs at my soul regarding Paul. I think back to my times of hardship and suffering. I try to deeply consider the genesis of the pain and suffering and find that so much of it was because I was only thinking of myself, my embarrassment, my failure, my loss, and my hurt feelings. Through the entire process, April was by my side every step of the way; offering encouragement. And yet, she was dealing with the same feelings I was experiencing, likely much worse because she was also dealing with the loss of her beautiful mom. My self-centeredness must have been so discouraging for April, yet she was a constant source of strength and hope.

I think of Paul sitting in this jail cell. He was cold, in chains, and knew he was close to death. He was not asking for sympathy or throwing a pity party. Instead, he was writing a letter of encouragement to his friend Timothy. Paul was thinking of others, trying to help others even in his darkest days. Content.

I am reminded of April's mother, Virginia Bryant. When she was battling cancer, she endured some very bad days—days of extreme weakness and nausea. When she was having these bad days and felt like complaining, she said she knew what she needed to do; she needed to go out and help someone, be it a disabled couple at church, a friend, or the lady working the photo counter at Walgreens. She knew the best way to make herself feel better was to concentrate on others rather than herself. The heart of Paul. The heart of Christ. Content.

Virginia Bryant was a beautiful woman, physically and spiritually. She truly had the heart of a servant and was a constant source of joy. She fought her cancer for close to five years. Just before her passing, this picture was taken of her. She knew the end was close at hand. She had peace and joy for she knew the blessings of this life and the blessings of the life waiting for her with "her Jesus." The family joyfully calls the picture "Content."

Content.

The second Bible…One day, I stepped into the minivan and saw something else that was worn out. On the seat was my daughter's Bible. Used for many years, the cover and binding was coming undone. Pages were bent, crimped, and torn. There were stains inside and out. Bookmarks were set at several different passages. The Bible had mistakenly been left out in the rain after a campfire devotional at a youth retreat. It had visited the "lost and found" table at church. Notes had been written in the margins. Verses had been highlighted. It was also temporarily misplaced during one of our moves. It had been used and was worn.

I think of Paul's request for his scrolls and parchments and wonder what they must have looked like. Do you think they were clean and pristine, or do you think they were dog-eared and worn? Did he scribble notes in the margins and draw arrows to the back of the page to continue a thought? Did he underline verses? Did he find different color inks and highlight verses? Did he loan out the parchments to friends and family? Were they water stained even though Paul tried to keep them under his cloak during a heavy rain? Do I dare ask, "Was there a tartar sauce stain on them from the time Paul was reading while sitting at a table eating fish sticks?" For some reason, I believe his parchments looked like the pink Bible—worn and used.

Wearing something out takes time, be it gloves or a Bible. It also draws you closer to something. You can't wear something out without contact, and you can't have repeated contact without being drawn closer to someone or something.

I think of the worn-out sports gear in the garage. It dawns on me that it is almost impossible to wear out sports equipment by yourself. You might say you can wear out running shoes by yourself, and you'd be right. You might also say the same for golf equipment, and while that technically is true, playing alone is less fulfilling. That's why there is the famous question asked to golfers, "If you could play in your dream foursome, who would you play with?" Reality is this: It takes time with other people to wear out baseball bats and gloves, basketball shoes, and footballs.

Time and proximity. Memories. Relationships.

Is that what life is all about? Is that what gives call to a life of value?

In the same way you can't wear out sports equipment by yourself, you can't wear a Bible out by yourself. You may be reading alone, but you're actually developing a relationship. Every worn-out Bible proclaims, "Come close to God and he will come close to you…"[134] It is time and proximity to God.

I look at a worn-out Bible and think of all that time and proximity with God. Isn't it amazing, the righteous and holy God of all gave us his Word because he wants a relationship with us? Our sovereign God desperately desires to share time and proximity with us lowly sinners, as he offers victory, love, and life.

Time and proximity.

I am a grandfather now, and I wonder if my son ever sits in his daughter's room and watches her sleep. Does he look at her face or watch her chest rise and fall with each breath? Does he look at her hands? Does he ever wonder if those hands will wear out gloves? Or better yet, will they be like the hands of the Apostle Paul and wear out a Bible?

Time and Proximity.

---

[134] James 4:8

Chapter 15

First Thorns

"It's not fair."

Friday, April 28, 2018, I write these words at 2:15 a.m. sitting in a wooden chair at Dallas Medical City Hospital. I am next to my mother's bedside. The open space on the mattress by her right leg is serving as the "desk" for my yellow legal pad. I had never dreamed this would be the setting for a portion of the writing of this book.

I had been planning on writing this chapter for many months, but for some reason, had never gotten around to creating the body of this text; it was simply a collection of quickly scribbled, somewhat illegible ideas. I had originally planned to write about my mother-in-law and the courageous journey she endured with cancer. It was a time she lived with incredible dignity, and her death was consistent with the way she lived, joyfully giving the fullest glory to God on high.

In reviewing my notes, the original introduction line for this chapter was "Cancer is not a fair fight." I think that is something with which we would all agree.

But I am sitting next to my mother, who has suffered a severe stroke, and the concept of fairness does not seem to limit itself to the ravages of cancer. This is not fair.

My mother had attended a women's Bible study on Wednesday morning, April 25. Their topic was "Choose Joy" and the Book of John, and she had commented to my dad that it was her favorite study, which said a lot considering her seventy-six years of constantly being in the Bible. From what we have been told, my mother had mentioned to a few of the ladies that she had a headache that morning, but she still participated and actually had some nice closing comments to the study. As is the custom, the ladies were having a luncheon to mark the end of the quarter and the study. She had just gotten her plate of food and was about to find a seat at one of the tables.

The particular type of stroke she had started with a brain bleed, and one of the symptoms would be feeling nauseous. Before she found her seat, she set her plate on a bench in the hall and entered the restroom. This restroom is used by brides and bridesmaids preparing for a wedding, so it is a nice, large restroom with a section that has seats and a small couch. Several minutes later, another woman entered the restroom and found Mom lying on the floor. An ambulance was immediately called, and she was able to softly tell people that her head was hurting. From the time she entered the ambulance to arriving at the hospital, the brain bleed had, in the words of the neurosurgeon, "exploded." She never regained consciousness. For all intents and purposes, she was brain-dead. Regretfully, there were no intentional last words with Mom, no long hugs or sweet "Goodbyes."

It's not fair.

The previous Thursday (April 19), my oldest son and his wife had a daughter. My wife and I had become first-time grandparents, and we were filled with immense joy. Six days later, around noon on Wednesday the 25th, we got the call about my mother and rushed from Oklahoma City to Dallas to be at her bedside. Three days later, at 2:54 a.m. on Saturday, Margie Stephenson (GranMom) passed from this life. For my wife and me, it was a short journey from immense joy to the fullness of sorrow. I guess it is true when they say, "Life is a roller coaster."

GranMom at a grandchild's wedding

GranMom was an extremely godly woman who modeled love and servanthood to everyone with whom she came in contact. During our time with her in the hospital, our family was visited by hundreds of friends and family. Her visitation and funeral were attended by more than eight hundred people. A wide variety of people paid their respects, from the strongest of Christians to people who held no religious beliefs. It did not matter. These were people who simply wanted to honor her life of love, friendship, and genuine unending servanthood.

There was one woman in particular who made a comment that has stuck with me. She was in her mid-eighties and had literally known my mother from the day she was born. She was a very strong and courageous Christian, who had personally dealt with many episodes of disappointment and exceedingly deep sorrow. While at the visitation, this tiny white-haired woman hugged me and said she didn't understand what had happened to Mom. She seemed so frail and weary. Between soft sobs, she said, "I believe in God and the righteousness of his decisions. He is always right. But I don't understand this one. I don't know why he would take Margie. This doesn't seem fair." While holding back tears of my own, silence was my only honest response.

Like the stroke that took Mom's life, I don't understand the cancer that took the life of my mother-in-law. She too was an amazingly godly and joyful woman. Why? Why do beautiful roses have such painful thorns?

I have written much about Paul and his requests to God to have his thorn removed. We do not know what Paul's thorn was or why he thrice made the request. We do not know if his "thorn" was physical, emotional, psychological, or spiritual. We simply know it was unpleasant and Paul thought life would be better without the pain, or inconvenience, it caused. God's answer was not to remove the thorn, but that Paul should concentrate on the full sufficiency of God's grace.

In all of God's creation, there are certain items I do not understand why they were created—mosquitos, rats, fire ants, the Scottish dish called "haggis," just to name a few.

You can add to that list thorns. What is the reason for a thorn?

Do you know when the first thorn is mentioned in the Bible?

The answer is found very early in the Book of Genesis. God created the earth, and it was formless and void. In chapter 1:3–27, God gave the earth shape, form, function, life, and purpose. God created all inhabitants of the earth, including man and woman. God created man and woman to have a life of endurance and longevity. He built them for eternity. And the Bible implicitly states that God enjoyed the relationship with his creation.

In chapter 3, we are introduced to Satan and evil. In the form of a serpent, Satan deceived Eve, and she took of the forbidden fruit. She gave it to Adam, and he too ate of the fruit—the fall of man. Sin has entered the world and created a separation between God and man. From that day forward, the earth and the relationship between God and man has never been the same. In deep sorrow, God had to remove Adam and Eve from the Garden of Eden for fear they would partake of the fruit of the tree of life.[135]

---

[135] Genesis 3:22

And to Adam he said, "Because you have listened to the voice of your wife and have eaten of the tree of which I commanded you, 'You shall not eat of it,' cursed is the ground because of you; in pain you shall eat of it all the days of your life; *thorns and thistles* it shall bring forth for you; and you shall eat the plants of the field. By the sweat of your face you shall eat bread, till you return to the ground, for out of it you were taken; for you are dust, and to dust you shall return.'"[136]

It is apparent that the thorn was a result of sin. The Garden of Eden never contained any thorns or thistles. It was a place of pure beauty and joy. The Garden of Eden was God's original intent. Thorns and thistles were not.

I have been considering the garden and the unpleasant advent of thorns and how the life and history of all mankind has been changed so drastically due to toil among thorns and thistles. Is there more to the story than meets the eye? Again, I ask for your generous liberty as I explore theological implications and ideas outside the writing of the Bible.

I think of the time Adam and Eve were in the garden. We do not know much about their lives except God liked to walk with them in the cool of the day.[137] It is often assumed Adam and Eve were there for only a few days or weeks before Satan successfully tempted Eve, but the truth is we don't know. They could have been there for days, weeks, months, or even many years.

While in the garden, how did God interact with them? The text says he would walk with them. Was God with them in spirit or in a cloudy mist? Or, as Adam and Eve were created in the image of God, did God take on the bodily form of an earthly man and physically walk with them in the garden? Was God able to touch and hug them? What was the intimacy level of their relationship?

---

[136] Genesis 3:17–19 (ESV)
[137] Genesis 3:8

Though the Bible does not say, I also wonder if any children were born to Adam and Eve while they were in the garden. My curiosity is piqued due to the words God used when describing Eve's punishment for her sin. Chapter 4, verse 16, says, "To the woman he said, 'I will greatly increase your pain in childbearing; with pain you will give birth to children. Your desire will be for your husband and he will rule over you.'" If Eve had never had children before this time, wouldn't God have just said, "Bearing children will be very painful"? Instead, he said, "I will greatly increase your pain in childbearing." Had Eve already had children born to her and was it virtually painless? Is that why God said he would increase her pain? I honestly do not know.

However, in considering these loose possibilities, I began to look at God and his relationship to man differently. I mentioned I am a new grandfather. I had always heard that the role of grandparent was very different from parent, but you don't truly understand it until you hold in your arms the child of your child. I wonder, *If God took on the image of man, did he ever hold a child of Adam and Eve in his arms? Did God ever whisper baby talk to a child of his child? Did God hold a child of his child and look deep into its eyes while holding back his own tears of joy?*

I think it is funny to watch a new parent explain to a grandparent how to hold their child. My wife and I raised four children and have held countless other babies in our lives. Yet, when our granddaughter was born, our son and daughter-in-law offered suggestions on where to place our arms and how to hold the baby. Instead of laughing at them or telling them they don't need to instruct us experienced parents, we simply understand they are speaking out of love for their child just the way we did so many years before. If God got to hold a child, did Adam and Eve try to tell him how to hold the baby? Did they suggest how he should hold his arms and how to gently rock the child to sleep? I do not know if that ever took place, but can you imagine that picture? All-consuming, all-encompassing love! I cannot begin to adequately form words on this page to describe the beauty and love of the pure relationship that was the Garden of

Eden. I can only think of the phrase "heaven on earth." It was wholly perfect. It was pure. It was God's intent.

There were no thorns.

Now, imagine the scene when Adam and Eve were removed from the Garden of Eden. Can you even begin to imagine the pain and sorrow God was experiencing? He had created heaven on earth for his beloved children. He enjoyed walking with them and being an intimate part of their lives. Now, they were being "kicked out of the house." Any parent who has ever had to deal harshly with a child can relate to the immense pain of disciplining one you love so dearly. There is no greater pain than seeing your child in hurt and despair. Did Adam or Eve ever tearfully, or angrily, exclaim to God, "This isn't fair!"? In response, did God say, "Adam, you know this was not what I intended"?

What was the mood of heaven? All of the heavenly beings must have known what was happening; they knew the sorrow of God with the fall of man. God knew the feeling of that fall before. Satan, who had once been one of them, was now wreaking havoc. Did any of the angels say, "I just can't believe Satan is doing this. He used to be one of us"? Was heaven full of disappointment and sorrow? Was there palpable anger at Satan?

Eden was empty. God was full of sorrow. Satan, the fallen angel, was laughing in glee.

We read later where Adam and Eve had two sons named Cain and Abel, grandsons of God you might say. During a dispute over an offering to God, Cain killed Abel.[138] When God was questioning Cain about the whereabouts of the slain brother, we encounter the infamous line, "...Am I my brother's keeper?"

If you are like me, you probably read that passage and think about God's anger and disappointment toward Cain. But do you ever consider the depth of God's sadness? Did God kneel at the spot where Abel lay dead and weep over this death and the beginning of the sin of murder that would plague humanity? In overwhelming grief, with hands and knees in the dirt, did God softly say, "This

---

[138] Genesis 4:8

is not what was intended"? Could God's words be heard over the laughter of Satan?

The evening news broadcasts another school shooting, this time at the Santa Fe High School in Texas where ten were killed. And Satan laughs.

This is only a couple of months after the shooting at Parkland High School in Florida where seventeen were killed. And Satan laughed.

The World Trade Center attacks of 9/11. Columbine. The gulf wars. The Khmer Rouge Regime. The world wars. The Holocaust. The Plague of Black Death. The crusades. Death. Destruction. Despair. Sorrow reigning down on humanity. And Satan is laughing through it all.

As we sat in the waiting room at the hospital dealing with the reality of the severity of my mother's stroke, one of my brothers said, "I am so mad at Satan right now." It was anger born of the fact that Satan loves sin and sickness. Those things exist only because of Satan and his desire to "kill, steal and destroy."[139] Cancer or a stroke was never the intent of the Garden of Eden.

God is the Creator of all, the sovereign and supreme Ruler of the ends of the universe and beyond, the King of all time and eternity. And in our times of grief and torment, we ask, "God, why do you allow Satan to mock you? Why do you put up with it? Why do you let Satan win?"

I am well aware mine is not an original thought. In fact, the writer of Psalm 74 asked the same question.

"The Psalm dates to the time of exile when Israel had been destroyed as a nation, the Promised Land devastated and the temple reduced to ruins."[140] This psalm, much like many psalms and other writings of the Bible, is born of confusion, disorientation, and pain. The Israelite people felt like they had been rejected by God.[141] The

---

[139] John 10:10
[140] *NIV Study Bible* notes. Page 861–862
[141] Psalm 74:1

writer described acts of violence and defilement against God and the people. The writer cried out:

> How long will the enemy mock you, O God? Will the foe revile your name forever? Why do you hold back your hand, your right hand? Take it from the folds of your garment and destroy them![142]

Isn't that what we cry for so often? "God, destroy Satan and remove this sadness and torment from the earth! Remove your hand from your garment, snap your finger, or blink your eyes, whatever it takes to unleash the destruction of Satan. Do it!"

We cry out when we see injustice.

We cry out when we see man's inhumanity to man.

We cry out when we experience pain and sorrow.

We cry out when we lose a job or our home.

We cry out during times of financial difficulty.

We cry out when our children experience pain and sadness.

We cry out from the hospital bedside of our mom.

Yet, God remains patient.

His patience is sometimes hard to understand. Sometimes, it feels like injustice or apathy. Sometimes it feels like separation. Sometimes it…feels like a storyline to a psalm.

I wish I could talk to the writer of Psalm 74. I'd ask him, "What changed?" I would ask that because he did something interesting in the midst of the cries for God to destroy the enemy. He wrote:

> But you, O God, are my king from of old; you bring salvation upon the earth. It was you who split the sea by your power; you broke the heads of the monster in the waters. It was you who crushed the heads of the Leviathan and gave himself as food to the creatures of the desert. It

---

[142] Psalm 74:10–11

was you who opened up springs and streams; you dried up the overflowing rivers. The day is yours, and yours also the night; you established the sun and moon. It was you who set all the boundaries of the earth; you made both summer and winter.[143]

In the midst of crying out to God for destruction of enemies, the writer remembered who God was. The writer turned his attention from his enemies and thorns and thistles and back to God. In the midst of crying out for God to act here on earth, the writer remembered that the earth belonged to God. He laid it all at the feet of God the Creator.

Isn't that what God asks of us all the time—concentrate on me, and bring everything to me, even if it means you will bring sorrow and anger with you? God says, "Bring me all you have. Bring me all of your emotions. Bring me all of your questions. I am big enough to handle it all."

The writer of Psalm 74 turned all of his hope and trust toward God. In verse 21 he wrote, "Rise up, O God,…" No longer was the writer's hope in an earthly temple built by human hands or the promised land. His hope was in God.

We read about that earthly temple later. In John 2, Jesus made his famous statement to the Jewish leaders, "Destroy this temple, and I will raise it again in three days." The leaders laughed as they thought he was talking about the earthly temple in Jerusalem, which had required forty-six years of labor and construction. The leaders did not know Jesus was saying, "Don't concentrate on what is earthly. Concentrate on me and my Father." Another way of saying it may be "Don't concentrate on the thorns on earth. Concentrate on the Eden God has waiting for you in heaven."

I consider the things that have happened in my life, the good, the bad, the roller coaster. When things are not going well, the temptation is to always think about earthly things and consider the fair-

---

[143] Psalm 74:12–17

ness of it all. Feelings of helplessness and vulnerability take hold. I cry out, "I need help." The writer of Psalm 121 also cried out when he wrote, "I lift my eyes unto the hills, where does my help come from? My help comes from the Lord who made heaven and earth."[144]

The writer of Psalm 124 continued:

> If it had not been for the Lord who was on our side when people rose up against us, then they would have swallowed us alive, when their anger was kindled against us; then the flood would have swept us away, the torrent would have gone over us; then over us would have gone the raging waters...
>
> Blessed be the name of the Lord,... Our help is in the name of the Lord, who made heaven and earth.[145]

I still do not understand it all. I read the words of James 2, and I admit I am not always joyful when facing trials and tribulations. Life can be hard and painful here on earth. Some are self-inflicted wounds; others are not.

I do not understand the concept of free will. I am amazed at the idea of God's self-control to allow us to make decisions that are not always in keeping with his will. We sin. We fall short. We willingly put ourselves in situations that cause us grief and harm. In some cases, God allows us to do so. And I believe in other cases, God may somehow intervene. Why and when? Who and how? I do not know.

The thorns that seem so hard to understand are the ones caused by others. Grief that lands at our doorstep because of the actions of others. Theft. Embezzlement. Lying. Drunk drivers. Rape. Murder. We cry out for God to intervene. We see disease and cry out. We see infirmities and cry out.

---

[144] Psalm 121:1–2
[145] Psalm 124:2–8

There is another voice that cried out loudly one day. The voice was that of Mary, the mother of Jesus. Taking on the sin of the world, her son, her child, was being nailed to a cross. He was sinless and innocent, yet he was experiencing a death that was meant to not only cause excruciating pain but also deep humiliation and shame. Death by crucifixion was a tool of the Romans to cause great fear among their enemies. Already severely flogged and beaten, Jesus would have been barely clothed, or naked, as he was laid bare on the cross in front of the world. Can you imagine? This was not fair. And Mary stood at the foot of the cross as Jesus declared "It is finished"[146] and breathed his last. Could she hear Satan laughing and mocking her Son?

God and the heavens cried out in grief and agony. God was watching his Son, and the angels were watching their friend and companion being humiliated and tortured. As the Father, if there was ever a time for God to remove his hand from the folds of his garment and destroy Satan, it was this day; it was to save his Son. However, we all know the story; Satan lived on and laughed. And from our deepest core we ask, "Why?"

When facing times of struggle and difficulty in understanding, I find great comfort in the words of the Apostle Paul in Hebrews 12:2:

> Let us fix our eyes on Jesus, the author perfecter of our faith, who for the joy set before Him, endured the cross, scorning its shame, and sat down at the right hand of the throne of God.

Maybe this is all the answer we need to the question, "Why?" Why would God allow this to happen to his beloved Son? Why would Jesus endure such indescribable agony and shame? Why is God so patient? The reason is ingloriously simple, "for the joy set before Him." The joy described here is the knowledge Jesus had of eternity in heaven with you and me. The future joy of spending eternity with you in heaven kept Jesus fixed on the cross when he could have called ten thousand angels to set him free. It is the same hopeful joy that kept God's hand in the fold of his garment. "Why?" seems

---

[146] John 19:30

to be all about you and me and the "New Eden" prepared for us in heaven. Let us fix our eyes on Jesus.

In times of justice and injustice, in times of fairness and unfairness, there are some constants:

- God loves you beyond anyone's ability to describe.
- God is good.
- God is faithful.
- God keeps his promises.
- We are not living in the Garden of Eden. We are in a fallen world. But, even though we are in a fallen world, there is still found indescribable joy and goodness.
- There are no thorns and thistles in heaven.

This gives me hope. I long for heaven and the peace and joy therein. I long for that day. But I keep asking myself, "What about... this day? What about today?"

I fix my eyes on Jesus as he hangs on the cross, and another lesson becomes very clear.

His body is beaten and bruised and pierced. He has breathed his last. His limp body is held up only by the nails in his hands and feet. The Son of God. Savior. Emmanuel. The King of kings is wearing a crown of thorns.

In dealing with hardships of life, it may be comforting to say, "Let us not concentrate on the earthly thorns of this life, but on the Eden that awaits us." However, my mind is now firmly fixed on the body of Christ and the thorns in the crown.

There is no denying each day is filled with thorns and thistles. It is reality. And like all things in life, I must choose what I do in that reality. What do I choose to do in the midst of thorns and thistles? As Christians, it is easy to cry out for God to take it all away. We know his power and unbridled authority. Even more so than the nonbeliever, I believe Christians often struggle with thorns because we know God can take them away if he so chooses. What do we do if we receive the same answer God gave Paul, "No, My grace is sufficient"? What then? What do I do in the thorns?

I am reminded of a famous line in the movie *The Shawshank Redemption*. Andy Dufresne has been wrongly accused of murdering his wife and her lover, and he has spent almost two decades in prison. His incarceration was not fair. After yet another act of cruelty by the warden, Andy has reached his mental breaking point. He is talking to his friend "Red" about getting out and moving to Mexico and the shores of the blue Pacific Ocean. Red, who does not know about Andy's plan to escape, discourages Andy as he is convinced this foolish thinking will only drive Andy further toward his breaking point. Frustrated, Andy finally says, "It comes down to one choice. You can get busy living or get busy dying."

We have the same choice. We live in a thorn-infested world due to sin. Life is often unfair and cruel. That is reality. And here is where our choice comes in. Do we sit paralyzed in self-pity and despair, angry at God for not removing all adversity and hardship? Are we afraid to do anything for fear of potential discomfort? Do we let anger eat away at our souls? Are we unable to find joy in anything as we prefer to instead concentrate on thorns and thistles? Or, in the midst of an often-difficult reality, do we "get busy living"?

"Let us fix our eyes on Jesus." Consider that statement. Think honestly and deeply about what it means to you personally, theologically, and metaphysically (the nature of being, existence, and reality). Try to put yourself in the mind of Paul as he wrote those words. Think deeply and theologically about what it meant to Paul in the context of his letter, but also in his life. Contemplate those words on a storm-filled sea as Peter climbed over the side of a boat.

"Fix your eyes on me." Isn't that what Jesus told Peter when asking him to step out of the boat and walk out to him on the water? Have you ever wondered why Jesus called Peter out on the water during a storm? Why didn't Jesus call him out when the water was calm and Peter could more easily keep his focus on Jesus? Isn't that what corporate team building coaches preach? "So that you don't immediately get discouraged and quit, first make goals that are easily accomplished; then move on to harder goals." Instead, Peter was attempting the "impossible" all while being battered by the wind and waves. Considering the implications, it would have been hard enough to walk on a calm sea, but can you imagine trying to walk while the wind is blowing you off balance and waves are crashing against your body and you're holding your hands up in front of your face to deflect the rain and blowing mist while you're trying to keep your eyes on Jesus?

The team building coach would tell Jesus he should have allowed Peter to do something easy so he could accomplish the goal. I wonder if Jesus would reply, "It was easy. All he had to do was keep his focus on me."

What was Jesus teaching Peter that day? What was Jesus teaching the eleven other disciples who stayed in the boat as they hung over the edge struggling to see what was happening on the water? "Look what can be accomplished in the midst of difficulty and strife, if you will just stay focused on me. Look what you can do in the middle of the wind, waves...and thorns. Difficulty and strife is inevitable, but look at what you can do."

"Let us fix our eyes on Jesus." How did Paul come up with that phrase? Do you ever think about the times the apostles sat around together and talked and told stories? How many nights did they sit by a fire and tell stories of Jesus and of their ministries after they had been blessed with the Holy Spirit?[147] These group meetings would have been so very important as these times of reflection and storytelling would have been incredibly encouraging not only to these men but also the women and children who were also listening. I wonder, *How many times do you think Paul asked Peter about that day on the water?* Over the years, as the requests to hear the story must have been in the hundreds, how good did Peter get at telling that story? Did he tell it with drama, with humor, with shock and awe? Did the other disciples chime in and laugh and tell about Peter climbing out of the boat and wondering what he was doing? As Peter was describing the trepidation and excitement of his foot hitting the cold water, can't you see Paul laughing and saying something akin to "Oh man, that would be so awesome!"? Did that story play into Paul's memory as he wrote his letter to the Hebrews? "Let us fix our eyes on Jesus."

What can you do in the midst of thorns? Jesus had a crown of thorns cruelly stuck on his head, the thorns pressed into his skin only

---

[147] Acts 2:1–4

stopping when they hit bone. The thorns created at the fall of man were fully on display at the redemption of all mankind.

What can you do in the midst of thorns? You can overcome. You can win. You can get busy living.

As Christians, we are created in the image of God.[148] We were created to be his earthly agents, his ambassadors,[149] his priestly beings to lead earth in worship,[150] and his royal representatives to lead the earth in honoring the King's wishes. So often, we are good about calling out to God to right the wrongs, to heal the hurting, to correct injustice; but we don't do anything about it. Many Christians are good about recognizing injustice, pain, and suffering; but his ambassadors must stand and act in the gap until he comes again. We as his ambassadors must "toil among the thorns."

Mom knew she was living in a fallen world full of thorns, but she also knew she didn't have to participate in a lower grade of living. She let the beautiful fragrant rose blooms block the view of the painful thorns hiding within. Without riches or fanfare, she was intentional in her choice to be a source of joy and love. She literally held the sick. She literally cared for the hurting. She literally attempted to right injustices. She literally fed the hungry. She literally clothed the poor. She literally welcomed the stranger.

She knew this fallen world was not the world God intended from the beginning. She knew the "New Eden" was on the other side of life, and God had a home prepared for her with a good view of his throne. But, while she was here among the thorns, she was busy living.

In disbelief, I stand next to mom's bed in the hospital room watching her take her last breath here on earth. It is a difficult time of contrasting thoughts. From a spiritual standpoint, as a family, we are so happy for Mom and her entry into heaven and being in the presence of Jesus. But our earthly hearts and minds are saddened to the core while we whisper to ourselves, "This is not fair."

---

[148] Genesis 1:27
[149] 2 Corinthians 5:20
[150] 1 Peter 2:9–10

I sense an amazing irony though. While we stand at her bedside watching her leave this life, I think of Mom as she is getting her first glimpse of heaven and the overwhelming joy she begins to experience. She is in the presence of Jesus and God Almighty—the singing, the praise, the worship, the joy, the colors, the brightness, the glory, and the angels. Mom was always talking about angels. In all of that, it may seem strange that I smile when I think that Mom gets to see the archangels Michael and Gabriel. I can't begin to imagine the questions Mom will have for them about their experiences she read about in the Bible. I wonder too if the apostles still get together in heaven and tell stories for all to hear. Maybe Jesus is there to jokingly tamp down some of the exaggerations, especially of Peter. I'm sure it is a time of joy and laughter and celebration. Will Mom sit and listen and laugh her contagious laugh? Is that the definition of "pure joy"?

As Mom enters the gates of heaven, I see her weeping and falling to her knees. It is a two-pronged response. On one hand, she is overwhelmed by the goodness and grace of God as she knows he promised through Christ's sacrifice to joyfully accept her to the banquet. It is weeping in pure joy. But I also know Mom's humility, and I can see her saying, "I am just a lowly servant. I don't deserve to be in this majestic glory. This is not fair." With nail-scarred hands, Jesus lovingly takes her by the hand and says, "Margie, this is what my Father intended from the beginning. There are no tears or thorns in heaven. Well done, good and faithful servant… Come and share in your master's happiness!"[151]

Blessed be the name of the Lord.

No more thorns!

---

[151] Matthew 25:23

For I consider that the sufferings of this present time are not worth comparing with the glory that is to be revealed to us.
(Romans 8:18)

Chapter 16

"Shake Well Before Using"
(Liminal Space...Continued)

He calls from the kitchen, "Is this salad dressing still good?"

After a slight hesitation in remembering if the family health insurance premium is up to date, the answer comes from the living room, "Just shake it up."

*****

In chapter 1, the concept of liminal space was introduced. This is a time where circumstances have changed and you are entering an unknown and transformational time in life. This can be associated with debilitating and difficult times of tragedy or pain or a time of excitement, hope, and joy. It is simply a time where "certainty" and "rules" of life have changed; and whether you like it or not, you are facing a new normal.

In grief, pain, and denial, efforts are made to hold on to the past, albeit unsuccessful. In fear and anxiety, one can shrink into the supposedly safe world of nonaction while ignoring new and painful realities. Overwhelming adversities mount; and the thought, or hope, that anything in life can ever be good again is dim at best. All that was certain is gone, and you are "shaken to the core."

On the other hand, some enter into liminal space with pure joy and excitement while anticipating this uncertain future. New job. New city. Marriage. Children. Opportunities. Intellectual growth.

They stride headlong into the unknown and treat it as a time to experience new things in life leading to emotional, spiritual, psychological, mental, and relational growth. Pulling the mask off the unknown is exhilarating.

We often associate liminal space with family, health, and jobs; but have you ever considered the liminal space created by a developing faith? The usual scenario is a child is brought up in the faith of their parents, which is also typically the faith of their parents. At a minimum, you are living in a faith that is two generations old; and it is comfortable and safe. Then, all that we call "life" happens. Circumstances and relationships may change, and we are forced to honestly and deeply examine our faith. Or we meet people and strive to provide answers when asked to explain our beliefs, and simple cookie-cutter answers are no longer acceptable. We contemplate and formalize our personal faith all while considering salvation and eternity. This is a monumental process. It is no longer simply the faith of our parents; it becomes our faith, and our salvation, if that is even "a thing." For many, it is a time of struggle, conflict, and altered thinking as wisdom and experience increases insight. And unfortunately, for some, the struggle results in rejecting faith altogether. For others, it is a time of great liberation and growth as they realize their faith is formally their own. It may be a new faith belief, or it may be a confirmation of the faith of their fathers, but it is theirs.

Have you ever considered how often and regularly Jesus thrust people deeply into liminal space? How he broke down the walls of "the normal" and introduced new and radical ideas? He constantly pressed his disciples to look at the world differently and see into a glorious expanse of his kingdom. And conversely, Jesus seemed to be in constant conflict with the religious leaders of the day as he told them they had become slaves to the safety and comfort of rituals and man-made legalistic traditions. It was often very uncomfortable, but Jesus wanted people to question everything and develop a deep personal faith in him and the Father.

The Sermon on the Mount is something we read with relative ease. Yes, fulfilling the ideals is difficult even in the twenty-first century; but we have been exposed to them all our lives, and the concept is not shocking, because even two thousand years removed, we know the speaker—we know Jesus. But imagine a Jew living under Roman rule listening in astonishment and shaking their head in disbelief to this absolute nonsense spouted by a carpenter who was conceived out of wedlock and raised in a poor and deeply unsophisticated town… and this guy was wanting them to "Follow me."

> Blessed are those who are persecuted for righteousness' sake, for theirs is the kingdom of heaven. Blessed are you when others revile you and persecute you and utter all kinds of evil against you falsely on my account. Rejoice and be glad, for your reward is great in heaven, for so they persecuted the prophets who were before you.[152]

> You have heard that it was said, "An eye for an eye and a tooth for a tooth." But I say to you, Do not resist the one who is evil. But if anyone slaps you on the right cheek, turn to him the other also. And if anyone would sue you and take your tunic, let him have your cloak as well. And if anyone forces you to go one mile, go with him two miles. Give to the one who begs from you, and do not refuse the one who would borrow from you.[153]

> You have heard that it was said, "You shall love your neighbor and hate your enemy." But I say to you, Love your enemies and pray for those who persecute you, so that you may be sons of your Father who is in heaven. For he makes his sun rise on the evil and on the good, and sends

---

[152] Matthew 5:11–12
[153] Matthew 5:38–42

rain on the just and on the unjust. For if you love those who love you, what reward do you have? Do not even the tax collectors do the same? And if you greet only your brothers, what more are you doing than others? Do not even the Gentiles do the same?[154]

Or how about these golden oldies throughout the gospels?

If anyone comes to me and does not hate his own father and mother and wife and children and brothers and sisters, yes, and even his own life, he cannot be my disciple.[155]

Then he will say to those on his left, "Depart from me, you cursed, into the eternal fire prepared for the devil and his angels. For I was hungry and you gave me no food, I was thirsty and you gave me no drink, I was a stranger and you did not welcome me, naked and you did not clothe me, sick and in prison and you did not visit me." Then they also will answer, saying, "Lord, when did we see you hungry or thirsty or a stranger or naked or sick or in prison, and did not minister to you?" Then he will answer them, saying, "Truly, I say to you, as you did not do it to one of the least of these, you did not do it to me." And these will go away into eternal punishment, but the righteous into eternal life.[156]

I am the way, and the truth, and the life. No one comes to the Father except through me.[157]

---

[154] Matthew 5:43–47
[155] Luke 14:26
[156] Matthew 25:41–46
[157] John 14:6

> If anyone would come after me, let him
> deny himself and take up his cross daily and fol-
> low me. For whoever would save his life will lose
> it, but whoever loses his life for my sake will save
> it. For what does it profit a man if he gains the
> whole world and loses or forfeits himself?[158]

"Are you insane? You're telling me I'm supposed to be happy when people hate me, let some guy smack me on both cheeks just before I give him my coat for free, love my enemies…but hate my mom and dad, and take care of sick poor people in prison and I can only get to our eternal God of Israel through you and to follow you I'm supposed to take up my cross? And by 'cross,' of course, you mean the same cross the Romans use to horrifically crucify, impale, and burn people on? Okay, well…uh, psycho, uh, how 'bout a big fat no thank you?" They would walk away from Jesus shaking their heads and saying, "This guy is out of his mind! He's a raving lunatic!" And yet, amazingly, some people heard those same words; and their minds and hearts were pricked, and they stepped into their liminal space.

Jesus pressed people further into the unknown with his rule-breaking actions. He walked through Samaria rather than around it. As a rabbi, he shockingly spent time with women in public, and some were even women of ill repute. He actually went into homes and ate with known "sinners" reviled by the town. And can you imagine the audible gasps when he touched a person with leprosy as they yelled the self-condemning cry of "I am unclean!"? As I type those words, I wonder if the loudest gasp was from the crowd or from the leper himself. Someone, who by no action of his own, was cast out of society. Dirty. Unclean. Friendless. In severe pain. He might have had a loving family whom he now must avoid for fear of transmitting the disease. Lonely beyond understanding. All-encompassing misery. And then this man touched him, on purpose. The leper would have gasped in terror as this happened. But can you

---

[158] Luke 9:23–25

also imagine how soul stirringly satisfying that simple touch was? All who witnessed it were forced into a liminal space. Jesus shook people to the core.

Chris Seidman, pulpit minister at The Branch Church, offered a sermon about "Isaiah" and had this wonderful synopsis about times of transition:

> *Usually God uses his people the most in times of transition. If you look in the Bible, God uses his people the most in times of great national and global turmoil, in times of great cultural transition. But here's the deal, if we are going to wake up and step up to God's open call to use us in these times, we have to have these convictions settled in; God is over it all, and God is in the middle of it all. And, God wants to cleanse us of it all.*
>
> *Four takeaways from Isaiah's open call.*
>
> *1. God often allows us to be shaken before being used. Open up your fridge and look at the salad dressing label. It says, "Shake well before using." That should be our motto. God has to allow us to be shaken, because being shaken is part of you growing into a greater awareness of God over it all, God in the middle of it all, and God cleansing us of it all. I'm more apt to step up and say, "Here I am. Send me."*
>
> *2. In times of great transition, we need a clear vision of God. If you live long enough, you're going to have a moment where Uziah's leave the throne and Assyria is on the rise, and in those moments of transition, you desperately need a clear vision of God over it all, in the middle of it all, and God cleansing it all. When I'm out of touch with the reality of God, I'm out of touch with reality. A clear vision of God will give you hope in times of transition.*

3. When God becomes heavier to us, we are more likely to move in response to Him instead of trying to move Him around. God needs to be the one moving us, instead of us trying to move him around.

4. We don't fulfill a calling in order to be cleansed, we fulfill a calling because we are cleansed. God cleanses Isaiah before allowing him to step up. If you have guilt, fulfilling a calling will not cleanse you of your sin, only God can cleanse you of your sin. That's why God has to bring the sacrifice to you in the altar. GOD CLEANSES THOSE HE CALLS.[159]

I love the image of shaking the salad dressing. We have all opened the fridge, looked at an expiration date, hesitated while wondering whether it was good or not, and then shaken the salad dressing and called it "good to go." It has been shaken, and the frigid bonds of settling have been broken.

In chapter 2, "Lost," I offered the description of a liminal space as entering "God's waiting room." I picture someone who is facing a new uncertainty and "shaken well" before walking into God's waiting room.

- Adam and Eve had sinned and must leave the beautiful Garden of Eden...[160]
- Noah was given blueprints for a boat...[161]
- Abraham was told he was going to be the father of a great nation, and he waited for twenty-five years...[162]
- Sarah overheard she was going to be a mother and laughed...[163]
- Joseph wore a colorful coat as he went to see his brothers. They captured him, threw him in a pit, and sold him to a

---

[159] Seidman, Chris. "Isaiah, the Calling." The Branch Church. (February 25, 2018)
[160] Genesis 3:22–24
[161] Genesis 6:14–16
[162] Genesis 12:2–3
[163] Genesis 18:12

passing caravan. He sat in the cart and looked back at his brothers...[164]

- Moses's mother shaped a floating crib and gently pushed him out into the river...[165]
- Moses took matters into his own hands and killed an Egyptian and then ran to the desert and sat by a well...[166]
- In disbelief, Joshua and Caleb heard the other ten spies say they couldn't take the promised land...[167]
- Gideon was told he had too many men...[168]
- Bathsheba took a bath on the roof...[169]
- Nehemiah was ridiculed and thrown into the cistern of Malchijah and sunk into the mud...[170]
- Uninvited, Esther prepared herself to go see her husband king and plead for her people...[171]
- A poor, young, virgin girl named Mary was told she was going to have a child by the Holy Spirit and he would be the Messiah, and she sang...[172]
- Mom and Dad stopped what they were doing when Mary nervously asked, "Can I talk to you about something?"...
- King Herod heard about the birth of the King of the Jews from the Magi...[173]
- Peter stepped over the rails of the storm-tossed boat...[174]
- Zacchaeus climbed a tree...[175]

---

[164] Genesis 37:12–30
[165] Exodus 2:3–10
[166] Exodus 2:15
[167] Numbers 13:31–33
[168] Judges 7:4
[169] 2 Samuel 11:2–27
[170] Nehemiah 38:6
[171] Esther 5:1–8
[172] Luke 1:26–38, 46–56
[173] Matthew 2:1–9
[174] Matthew 14:27–31
[175] Luke 19:2–9

- She passed the disciples as she ran back to town after talking to a man by the well...[176]
- Jesus wrote in the dirt with his finger...[177]
- Her parents told Jesus her name was Talitha...[178]
- A widow humbly gave her last two coins...[179]
- Thirty pieces of silver richer, Judas walked out into the cold night...[180]
- Mary wept as her child was nailed to a cross...[181]
- They gathered in an upper room with the door locked...[182]
- On his hands and knees, a blinded Saul felt the hard dirt of the road to Damascus. He would live in darkness for three days...[183]

I think of Paul and his darkness for three days and obviously see the similarity to Jesus in the tomb. Have you ever considered that the three days Jesus spent in the tomb was the greatest liminal space of all time? Whether or not people understood it, Jesus had entered God's waiting room, and *everything* had changed. All the rules had changed. There was no "normal" remaining, either on earth or in heaven. It was as if the entire universe of all heaven and earth had gone with Jesus into God's waiting room.

"Shake well before using." Obviously, Jesus was useful his entire life, but the night in the Garden of Gethsemane was a time of incredible upheaval for him. He knew of the physical suffering about to befall him. He knew the incredible pain and difficulty his friends, the disciples, were going to face in the next few days. He wept for the soul-deep sorrow his mother Mary was going to experience in seeing him beaten and nailed to the cross. But his greatest pain was

---

[176] John 4:1–32
[177] John 8:1–11
[178] Mark 5:35–43
[179] Luke 24:1–4
[180] John 13:30
[181] John 19:25–27
[182] John 20:19
[183] Acts 9:1–19

in knowing he would take on all the sin of the world and be separated from his Father during this time. In Chris Seidman's takeaways, he mentioned an "awareness of God over it all, God in the middle of it all, and God cleansing us of it all." Jesus was going to be separated from God in the middle of it all, and the pain overwhelmed him. Beyond the physical earthquake occurring during his crucifixion, his life, death, and resurrection spiritually, emotionally, and culturally "shook the world before using."

Jesus shook people to such a degree that many watched him out of simple morbid curiosity. Many quit following him due to his bizarre words and actions. Many wanted to kill him as a threat to their safety and security. And some never wanted to leave his side.

Being in the liminal space can be very difficult, but it can also lead to tremendous growth. When the persecution against Christians increased in ferocity, the Christians had a few choices; they could leave their homes and go somewhere safer, they could stay and profess their love for Christ and likely be killed, or they could deny Christ and live. Take some time and truly consider what these men and women faced. They were staring deep into that liminal space, entering the unknown, entering uncertainty all based on this man they had known for only a short period of time. This not only affected them; it affected their entire families and especially their children. Did they profess Christ and put their lives and their children's lives in peril? Imagine the agony of their decisions.

Many ran and lived. Many stayed and died. Many stayed and lied.

Isn't it amazing that this time period was one of the strongest periods of Christian growth in the world? Those who left spread the gospel around the world. The ones who stayed and died were an amazing witness to the loyalty and dedication of the Christians. Think of the impact it had on people who watched them being killed, as those people had to be asking themselves, "What is it about this man Jesus that would make them give up their lives to profess his name?" And the church grew in the middle of stunning adversity.

It is also amazing to see how perceptions of liminal space can be so contradictory. As Jesus's body was nailed to the cross, Satan and his minions were rejoicing in their apparent victory, while all of heaven bowed its head in sorrow. But, three days later, on the other side of it, the roles were completely reversed as Christ was declared the victor.

"Shake well before using." Do we look at the times in our lives when we faced difficulties and were shaken as opportunities to grow? When the liminal space is unexpected, unwanted, and/or undesirable, being shaken can be discouraging! You feel defeated and weak. You feel dizzy and unstable, and things are out of focus. That was why Jesus told Peter to keep his eyes on him in the storm and not look at the waves of deceit, doubt, and distraction tossed by Satan. "Focus on me," he said. "And look... You're walking on water!"

Choosing to enter an unknown and being shaken can also be exhilarating! I was in Southeast Idaho working on a golf course project and came across a historical marker sign along a highway. It was the story of a famous trapper and explorer who was with a group of men when a fast-moving blizzard hit. Everyone began looking for safe cover, but the famous trapper began to climb a large tree. All the other team members were incredulous and asked what he was doing. Reaching for the next branch, he replied, "I want to experience everything about a blizzard." The men found shelter knowing their friend would likely die in the elements. All the men, including the trapper in the tree, survived the storm; and one came out on the other side with a great story to tell.

When our blizzards hit, do we seek shelter or climb a tree? When our lives are shaken, do we fear what will happen next, or do we step into the unknown with a hope and "awareness of God over it all, God in the middle of it all, and God cleansing us of it all"? And, in the middle of it all, we must search our soul and remember God is showering us with an all-sufficient grace and telling us "I can do great things with you and your weakness."

It took a storm for Peter to climb out of the boat.

It took blindness for Paul to see what it meant to be content.

It took Jesus's death to have a resurrection and salvation.

It took a blizzard to create a story from the branches of a tree.

What is your story?

> But in your hearts set apart Christ as Lord. Always be prepared to give an answer to everyone who asks you to give the reason for the hope that you have. But do this with gentleness and respect. (1 Peter 3:15)

> Therefore we do not lose heart. Though outwardly we are wasting away, yet inwardly we are being renewed day by day. For our light and momentary troubles are achieving for us an eternal glory that far outweighs them all. So we fix our eyes not on what is seen, but on what is unseen. For what is seen is temporary, but what is unseen is eternal. (2 Corinthians 4:16–18)

Chapter 17

Scars

How do you finish a book?

I've often heard the beginning and ending of a book are the hardest to write. As a first-timer, I would agree wholeheartedly. I am not a skilled writer, and searching for an appropriate end has been a struggle. Disappointment set in after numerous attempts to close with some witty wordplay or life-altering words of wisdom. It was not until I heard one of my sons preach a sermon on Easter morning that I found the closing to a book about trying to find joy and meaning in struggles and seeking contentment.

From the pulpit of Brooks Stephenson:

> It was only several hours, but it was a whirlwind of betrayal, mockery, deceit, and torture. Jesus lifeless body is removed from the cross. Only a faithful few of Jesus' followers remain, and they ask for the body and prepare it for burial.
>
> The Jewish leaders have pulled it off. Afraid to lose their power and influence, they scheme and connive their way into having an innocent man arrested, flogged, and crucified on a cross. Their callous display of power was brazenly public. You would think they would be satisfied, but they are not. They want to make sure this battered body will rot long in the tomb, and the

225

smell of his death to permeate the graveyard and testify to all who dare challenge their authority.

The Jewish leaders ask the Roman authorities for the tomb to be guarded. Pilate obliges and post some of his most skilled warriors to keep Jesus' followers from robbing the tomb and claiming Jesus had risen.

Jesus is dead. His body lies in the dark tomb sealed with a stone and guarded by Roman soldiers. How did this happen? He said He was the Messiah, but what do we make of him now?

What about the followers of Jesus? Where do they go from here? Their entire lives, and their longing hope, have been placed on this man just crucified. What now?

The next day is the Jewish Sabbath; the day in which all of Jesus followers are required by God's law to stay and rest. What were they thinking? How was Peter dealing with his sword play in the Garden of Gethsemane, and three angry denials by the fire? What images and sounds from the cross were burned into the minds of Mary Magdalene and John? How was Jesus mother, Mary, dealing with the grief and horror of watching her Spirit breathed Son being tortured and literally nailed to a contaminated blood stained wooden cross? What does that do to a mom?

Oh, if they could just get busy and occupy their minds. Did they long to unmoor their boats and find solitude fishing in the deep water, far away from the accusing eyes of the townspeople? Did they want to get on their horses or donkeys and ride hard for a few days to get away from this place of death? Anything.

But they had to wait and rest. Wait and reflect. They wait and wonder what the last few years were really about. Was there any truth in it at all? Was it all a con? Was he really the Messiah? What do they make of the man lying in a dark tomb?

They wonder if their families are going to be okay, or will the Jewish leaders round them up and have them killed as well? They wait, but rest is a stranger. They wait, and hope for some sort of absolution in their minds.

Then, we read in John 20:1, "Early on the first day of the week, while it was still dark, Mary Magdalene went to the tomb and saw that the stone had been removed from the entrance." Mary runs and tells the disciples and they come to the empty tomb to see for themselves, but they still don't understand the scriptures of Jesus being raised from the dead.

Distraught, confused and scared, the disciples hide in a room behind a locked door. Miraculously, Jesus appears in the midst of the room. This man who had been brutally beaten and crucified has now, somehow, come through locked doors and is standing in front of them; alive. Is this really Jesus? Luke writes that the disciples "were startled and frightened and thinking they saw a ghost."[184] And Jesus said to them, "Why are you troubled, and why do doubts rise in your minds? Look at my hands and my feet. It is I myself! Touch me and see: a ghost does not have flesh and bones, as you see I have."[185] The gospel writers tell of joy and amazement as the disciples see and touch the scars and realized it truly was Jesus.

---

[184] Luke 24:37
[185] Luke 24:38–39

But, there was at least one disciple who was not hiding behind locked doors, and did not see Jesus; Thomas. After several days, the disciples are together again and they are telling Thomas, "We have seen the Lord!"

Can you imagine the emotional and spiritual roller coaster the last week has been? Before the Passover week, the disciples do not want to go to Jerusalem for fear of what might happen to Jesus. They enter the town to people laying palm branches down and joyfully proclaiming his authority as they shout Hosanna![186] Jesus angrily clears the temple. He meets with people. He heals people. He debates leaders. He has a last supper with his disciples. He goes to a garden to pray. Judas arrives with a large company of Roman soldiers. Peter wants to fight and die with Jesus, but Jesus tells him to stop and put his sword away. Fear and confusion grip the disciples and they run from Jesus' side. He is alone. He is killed. He is placed in a tomb.

Thomas had been on this rollercoaster with the other disciples. For reasons unknown, he was not with the disciples when Jesus first appeared. And now, he is hearing this incredible news second hand? Is it any wonder Thomas has some doubts?

Thomas saw, or at least heard about, Jesus being put on trial, beaten, crucified and buried behind Roman guards. Thomas was with Jesus during his ministry. He walked with Jesus, formed a relationship with Jesus, shared meals and jokes and deep conversation with Jesus. Thomas is surely deep in grief as he tries to deal

---

[186] Mark 11:9

with the fact that his Rabbi, his Teacher, his Mentor, his Leader, his Hope, his Friend is no more. And then, he gets hit with, "We have seen the Lord!" Is it any surprise Thomas has some doubts? I wonder, did the other disciples sense his doubt and reassure him by saying, "Thomas, we were so scared. We thought he was a ghost, and then he showed us the scars on his hands and feet, and where the spear had been thrust into his side." We do not know how the disciples told the news, but we are all familiar with Thomas reply, "Unless I see the nail marks in his hands and put my finger where the nails were, and put my hands into his side, I will not believe."[187]

A week later, Thomas and the disciples are again gathered behind locked doors. Suddenly, Jesus appears to them. He looks at Thomas and says, "Put your finger here; see my hands. Reach out your hand and put it into my side. Stop doubting and believe." Listen to Thomas response this time, "My Lord and my God!"[188]

This is basically how the Gospel of John ends. A call to belief in the risen Messiah.

And this too is where we tend to stop. But have you ever wondered, "What is Jesus doing with those scars?" Isn't he resurrected? Isn't he supposed to be redeemed, restored, and made whole? Is the resurrection not what we had hoped for? If Jesus is going to be restored and made whole, shouldn't he be pure, holy, and made completely new again? Wouldn't skin pure as a newborn baby show power over all the effects of death and the darkness of Satan? Is this heaven

---

[187] John 20:25
[188] John 20:28

thing of no pain a sham? Why isn't anyone who sees the resurrected Jesus asking about his scars?!

Perhaps... Perhaps the most interesting thing to observe in all of this is that Jesus himself is the one who draws attention to His wounds. He is not afraid of showing his scars to his followers. In fact, Jesus acts like it is totally natural.

I read this account and have questions. I wonder about the scars. I sense Jesus saying to me, "No Brooks, my power is not insufficient to heal my wounds." Could you imagine that? Can you imagine Jesus saying, "Yeah, I have the ability to raise myself back to life, but these darn holes in my hands and my side, I just can't seem to figure out how to clear those things up." I wonder instead if Jesus would say, "Brooks, I have the power to remove the scars, but they serve a purpose. I need to be able to prove to the disciples who I am and what I have the power to do. These scars may not be pretty, but they show what I have the power to overcome. I have overcome death."

The presence of Jesus scars do not condemn him as one who is not powerful; instead, it is proof that He is! Each scar proclaims the power to turn the worst in human suffering into the most God-glorifying experience you and I could ever imagine. He would go on to give his followers the ability to understand just what his death and resurrection accomplished for them, as made obvious by their words and actions for the rest of the New Testament, but the message started here. "Sure, I suffered, I died, I was brutally and undeservedly beaten just like you saw...but through it, God was working and bringing about new life in me! And those same scars are convincing you of my power here and now. Come and see how I suffered and see that I can give you life even in the midst of your suffering."

Jesus wanted to show his scars to those in the room.

Who all was hiding in the room behind locked doors? Was it all the disciples? Were there others? Were there women like Mary Magdalene in the room? Were the wives and children of the disciples there? Was Peter's mother-in-law there? Who all was there? Was the room crowded enough that someone had to stand on their tip toes to be able to see Thomas touching the scars of Jesus?

If you were there, wouldn't you be curious too? Wouldn't you ask Jesus if you could maybe take a little peek? Would you dare ask to touch the scars yourself? Why? What would it do to your soul and your mind to feel the unevenness and impurity of those scars under your smooth fingers?

History tells us the impact it had on some who were in the room. James would later be beheaded for his faith. Peter and Andrew would be crucified. Even our good friend Thomas is believed to have died a martyr's death. Numerous other accounts exist of persecution, banishment from towns, imprisonment, floggings, and exile. I wonder how many of these individuals in the midst of their suffering thought back to the hands and side of Jesus and thought, "I know this can turn out for someone's good." Or, think about the opposite side of it all. How often did people watch what was happening and ask, "Why are these people so different? Why are they willing to suffer like this?"

Have you ever considered the amazing reaction of Pilate? He represents Rome as its leader. He is all powerful. He, like most Roman leaders, is ruthless and uncaring. He would sentence people to death and never think twice about it. Ordinary people meant nothing to him. Except for the desire to keep peace so the Jewish people could provide food for Rome, the Jewish people meant nothing to him. And now, in front of him stands a lowly Jewish carpenter, an absolute nobody. For Pilate, deciding what he wanted for breakfast might take more mental energy than deciding the fate of this meaningless man from the meaningless town of Nazareth. And yet, Pilate knows there is something different about this man. Pilate has heard of this man and his curiosity gets the best of him. He asks Jesus some questions, to which Jesus gives answers that cause even more curiosity. Finally, Jesus stands silent and refuses to offer a defense. Pilate is amazed. He summons the Jewish leaders and asks again why they want to kill this man. Pilate declares that this man has done nothing wrong. "This man doesn't deserve this." "What you are asking me to do doesn't make any sense." Imagine the magnitude of the fact that Pilate, the powerful Roman leader, is bargaining for the life of this "nobody from nowhere." Why?

Did word leak out that Pilate was trying to save Jesus? Did rumors spread throughout the crowd that Pilate might release him? If there were followers of Jesus hiding in the crowds, where they joyful in hearing that Jesus may be set free?

It was all for naught. Fear and politics eventually got the best of Pilate and Jesus was led to the cross, and rusty nails, and the dark tomb.

Then, there were new rumors spreading through the town. Could it be true? Is He alive? How could it be? The people saw Jesus' flesh torn from his body as a result of the flogging. They saw nails driven into his hands and feet. They saw the Roman soldier thrust the spear into Jesus' side. They saw his blood-soaked limp body fall to the dirt at the foot of the cross when he was taken down. They saw...and after the resurrection, Jesus invited them to look even more. Look at the scars.

The fact that Jesus bears the wounds of His crucifixion even after his resurrection is not bad news. On the contrary, it might be some of the best news that you and I could ever receive. *Even our suffering matters!* We've all been there, or will be. Those situations in our lives when we think, "What's the meaning of this?" "Why do I deserve this?" Or, "How could anything good come out of this?"

Jesus scars testify to unfairness. And yet, it is that exact suffering; those same wounds that cause all of these followers to believe and understand the power of Jesus Christ.

Could your suffering do the same? If God was working in Jesus' wounds, could He work in ours as well if we would let him? Could it be that there are some people who are watching you and I struggle and suffer in the world who would come to know the love of Jesus Christ if they could see how God is working through your scars? Instead of hiding my struggle and bearing the burden of it alone, if I let someone else see and even touch my wounds like Jesus did, could it lead to them turning to Jesus and saying, "My Lord and my god?"

A friend turns their back on you and starts spreading lies and rumors to those you love… "Why do I deserve this? What is the meaning of this?"

A job is lost seemingly out of nowhere and time goes on and on, and opportunity after opportunity arises but falls just a bit flat, and it's years of striving and pushing forward and working hard and asking, "How could anything good come of this? Why do my family and I deserve this?"

A doctor solemnly walks back into the room and confirms our worst fear. It's cancer and things don't look good. Treatment starts and the patient is losing strength, is constantly sick, and just wants to have a normal day, if they can even remember what that means. "How could anything good come of this? What's the meaning? Why do I deserve this?"

"What is the meaning of this?" "How could anything good come of this?" Or, "Why do I deserve this?" Questions generally not born in the joyful times of our lives. But, is it possible to take heart knowing the events leading to the literal salvation of our souls were surrounded by these same painful questions? Life and hope born from scars.

Our suffering can have meaning, because even though He suffered, He rose, and He lives. Sometimes we have scars not because of something we did, but because of the actions of others. It seems so unfair. Why should I have these scars? Jesus suffered at the hands of others. His scars are there because someone fashioned thorn filled limbs into a mocking crown. His scars are there because someone held a whip, some nails, a hammer, and a spear. It seems so unfair, but even so, Jesus proved that good can come from scars. He suffered. He lives. He saves. By his scars, we win.

(Sermon delivered on April 21, 2019)

*****

"Never let them see you sweat" was a famous marketing line in the 1980s for an antiperspirant. But we have adapted the motto to all of life. We might be dying inside with conflict and anxiety, but we always tell people, "I'm fine." We are taught to hide any signs of struggle or failure, because doing so means you are weak or unable. Marriage difficulties, financial hardships, addictions, depressions, lust, jealousy, abuse, low self-esteem—these are all scars that our society and, unfortunately, many of our churches tell us are supposed to be kept hidden.

- We pray for God to change our difficult circumstances, rather than praying that God will change us and give us strength to deal with the circumstances in a manner in which he will be glorified.
- Instead of seeing our struggles as an opportunity to grow in faith and trust, we wonder why God is punishing us, and we look past the cross of Christ as we question his love.
- We struggle and fight and plan and scheme for earthly ways to change our current condition, rather than trusting and turning our lives over to a faithful God and asking him to lead us to the point on the other side he desires for us.
- When weak and hurting, we hide behind a mask of bravado.
- Instead of using our difficulties as a way to teach and encourage others who are going through similar trials and tribulations, we throw them no lifeline while they struggle and slip deeper into the quicksand we recognize so well.
- We hide our scars as shame, rather than using them as tools to glorify.

Sipping on hot morning coffee, I was reading Philippians 4:11–13 again, reading about contentment and the power to do all things—passages I had read many times. Only, this morning, the next verse caught my eye. Paul wrote:

Yet it was good of you to share in my troubles.[189]

In this passage, Paul was thanking the church in Philippi for their gifts and support of his ministry. But, this morning, the picture of a weight being lifted off of someone's back came clear to my mind. I saw an image of a burden being lifted by a community of believers; or was it a collection of angels? I could see no faces, but I saw strength in community and overwhelming relief on the one burdened. I saw a sharing of faith and encouragement. I saw Jesus showing Thomas his scars.

Physical scars can be embarrassing, ugly, disfiguring, and distracting. They give testimony to pain and suffering. But there is another phenomenon about scars I find interesting; they promote curiosity. Have you ever seen a scar on someone's body and you try to figure it out? As an athlete, I easily recognize the scar of a torn ACL (anterior cruciate ligament) on a knee or on the forearm of a baseball player who has had Tommy John surgery. It is easy to ask that person about the injury and subsequent surgery. It's sports talk, and often, the person likes to talk about it. And have you ever noticed that when you ask someone about a scar from a sports injury, there is always someone else who wants to show their scar? It almost becomes a competition of who has the biggest scar and best story of suffering. There are the glorious scars from the blown-out knee caused by a vicious tackle while diving across the goal line for the winning touchdown and the laughable scar from the time at the batting cage when trying to help someone with their swing and they inadvertently got hit with the bat in the forehead just above the right eyebrow and required eleven stitches. Misery loves company.

---

[189] Philippians 4:14

But there are many scars that are not easily visible, and we prefer to keep it that way. A bruised ego. A broken heart. A crushed spirit. A weak faith. A lost soul. Human failings. The scar caused by the belief that your sin has cast you far beyond the reach of God's grace. Surely nobody wants to compare scars like these. Right?

For years, I hid my scars fearing that it might be possible for someone to hear our story and make me feel even worse about myself than I already did. But, when we moved to a new city, some people knew who I was and would ask why we were there. I slowly began to open up and tell bits and pieces. As I would tell our story, many people would begin to cry and tell me about their scars. People would say they were going through the same things and didn't have the courage or know how to seek guidance or counsel. They were embarrassed to ask for prayers. They were ashamed and frightened to tell their spouse and children that they were hurting so deeply. Women would ask me how April was staying so strong in the midst of the storm. Men, almost seeking a miracle cure, would ask me what I had done to get through it all. I tell them I'm still in the middle of it, but I am seeking contentment and trying every day to trust God because he is faithful. I pray for his strength to reveal my scars.

I close with the words of Tony Coleman, an Oklahoma City pastor and attorney:

> There was turmoil, chaos and confusion, but then he rose!
> There was sickness, disease and famine, but then he rose!
> There was death, destruction and darkness, but then he rose!
> We were lost, misguided and deceived, but then he rose!
> He was bruised, wounded, chastised, spat on, whipped, beaten, mocked, crucified and buried,
> *But with scars he then rose with power over it all.* Amen!

"He himself bore our sins" in his body on the cross,
so that we might die to sins and live for righteousness;
"by his wounds you have been healed."
(1 Peter 2:24 NIV)

But he was pierced for our transgressions,
he was crushed for our iniquities;
the punishment that brought us peace was on him,
and by his wounds we are healed.
(Isaiah 53:5 NIV)

About the Author

Gary Stephenson is a golf course architect and land planner who has designed more than thirty-five courses throughout the United States and internationally in Thailand, Mexico, Australia, and Scotland. He has worked in a wide variety of climates and terrains and has successfully designed golf courses in some of the most environmentally sensitive areas of the world. His Tierra Verde Golf Club in Arlington, Texas, was awarded as a prestigious Audubon International Signature Sanctuary. Five of his courses have been used as venues for professional golf tournaments.

In addition to a BS in biology (Lubbock Christian College, 1987) and a BS in park administration and landscape architecture (Texas Tech University, 1990), he earned a master's in Bible and family ministry from Lubbock Christian University in 2016. Gary is a popular Bible teacher, preacher, and featured speaker at youth retreats and men's events.

Gary and his wife, April, are blessed to live in Oklahoma close to their four married children and two beautiful granddaughters.

CPSIA information can be obtained
at www.ICGtesting.com
Printed in the USA
LVHW012248210721
693344LV00002B/4